THE
HYENAS

CHARLIE SEIGA

SPELLING DIFFERENCES: UK V US

This book was written in British English, hence US readers may notice some spelling differences from American English: e.g. color = colour, meter = metre and jewelry = jewellery

For Karen

A wonderful lady who gave me great inspiration
and encouragement regarding my writing.
I will be eternally grateful to her.

CONTENTS

PROLOGUE

The dreaded darkness is once again upon me. Sleep overwhelming me, no matter how hard I fight it. I know I can't hold out much longer. Maybe it's the comforting fire making me so drowsy. I lit it over an hour ago, but now it's reduced to a few glowing embers.

My brothers and I seem to be in the heart of a jungle. They are both fast asleep on either side of the fire, tightly wrapped in blankets, only their small heads visible.

I *must* stay awake, I can't let any harm come to my brothers - they are my responsibility. The words instilled into me by my parents echo in my mind:

'Charlie, you are the eldest and the strongest, take care of them.'

I tell myself to stay awake, though sleep is enticing me. I force myself to sit upright, resting my back against the trunk of a big solid tree, in the hope that it will combat the drowsiness. But it doesn't help and I feel my body succumb to the familiar paralysis.

'Don't worry,' I tell myself, 'I have my faithful knife.'

I am always tooled up and, out of all the weapons I have ever used, the knife remains the weapon of choice for me; it's silent and swift; no fuss. Knives are easy to get rid of and have none of the identification marks of a gun. No harm will come to my brothers; I'll make sure of that.

But then it comes again, in waves this time, the dreaded darkness. My head begins to roll, but again I pull it up and in that instant... I see it! A big hideous beast is walking slowly and silently out of the dark jungle, towards the fading light of our camp. I see only its eyes and the cavern of its mouth, saliva dripping to the grass below. I'm paralysed. Or am I? I try to shout, to warn my brothers, but my voice is just a low whisper. The hyena looks over at me, its yellow eyes staring straight into mine. In the past, I have looked many a man straight in the face and stared them out, but the look from this animal is too intense for me.

I try to tear my eyes away from its evil gaze but feel frozen, forced to observe the beast. It stops in its tracks, its horrible eyes moving to my innocently sleeping brothers. It glances back at me almost taunting, as if saying, 'Just try to stop me!' It creeps quickly over the ground between us, until it stands over my younger brother's innocent body.

Frantically, I scramble on the ground for my knife, eventually reaching it and getting my fingers around the handle; I try to lift it, but I just don't have the strength. Then it happens the hyena's face contorts into an almost human grin, twisted and wicked, then, in a swift movement it howls a terrible hideous note and tears at my brother's face. In one smooth motion the hyena holds the full face of my brother in its teeth. With shrieks of laughter the hyena twists around and kicks and runs back towards the quiet trees to hide its sins, my brother's face still in its mouth.

Suddenly, I am released from the spell and find my voice. I scream with fear. My body is stiff and my eyes are bursting out of my head, I breathe in short, sharp bursts and try with all my might to turn away from the sight of my brother's bloody, twisted body, twitching in the darkness...

I wake up screaming and gasping for breath. I struggle in my bed, at the sweat and sheets, at the air around me, at the darkness and the dream; this same dream night after night; without fail, without mercy. Once again in the darkness, I resolve to be stronger than before, to be faster than before, and to put an end to this. Of course, this was going to affect me. I couldn't just forget about it. But I had been strong where others would have been weak, had held out where some men would have broken. Remembering this makes me certain this lowlife scum can be beaten. And so it begins; a trail that takes me to the homes of men, women and children where I see first-handed the injuries these sick bastards gave them. My friends and I decide that we have taken just about enough of this fuckin' scum.

There was only one thing for it... they had to go.

CHAPTER 1

My name is Charlie Seiga. Armed robberies on banks and security vans, safe-breaking, hijacking lorries and many other serious crimes were once a way of life for me. I have been charged with grievous bodily harm several times, as well as 'threats to kill', attempted murders and murder. I've been a villain, or gangster, throughout my life. Obviously, I was no angel, and neither were my Firm or associates.

In those days, all my friends were men of honour. Believe it or not, there has always been a class distinction between villains. We never beat up old men or defenceless women. Of course, there have been times when we did hurt people; *really* hurt them, but they all deserved it, because they were women-beaters, muggers and lowlife scum. I have been fighting this type throughout my life. I can look back now on the villains I've known, and the villain I've been, and think how times and people have changed.

The villains I knew in the past had good principles. They say principles don't feed you, but I always believed in having respect and values. These days, there just seems to be none of that left. It's like dog eat dog. I think the drug game is playing a big part in it all, too. I've seen all the back stabbing going on and all the ripoffs happening. There just doesn't seem to be any trust left at all.

Some time ago, a woman came to see me. She was broken-hearted over her teenage daughter. I think the girl was about 17 or 18. It appears she had been set up on a drug deal. Apparently, some drug-dealer had sent her to Holland to pick up a kilo of weed and to bring it through Customs. Don't ask me how these people persuade young girls to do this for them. Maybe they have a hold on them somehow. Anyway, on the same return flight, the dealer also had another girl, only this one was carrying 1kg of pure heroin, a lot more valuable than the weed. Incidentally, neither of girls knew each other. When they finally arrived back in England, the girl carrying the weed was informed upon, and captured by Customs. Basically, this prick had used her as a decoy so that the other girl could get through with the more valuable drug.

A few months after this incident, the scumbag dealer was found dead in the flat where he lived. He had overdosed on the very poison he was peddling. It was a well-known fact amongst his fraternity that he was a keep fit fanatic and never took drugs himself. *'I wonder how that came about. Had somebody done him in?'* There's one good thing that has come out of it all; he won't be corrupting any other young kids with his filth.

Criminals of today are just not the same breed as we were. For example; when my friends and I were bang at it (into serious crime) we had rules amongst ourselves; rules that were never broken. Firstly, if any of our crew ever came unstuck on a piece of graft (criminal activity) the rule would be; you never roll over (make a deal with the police or inform) on the rest of the Firm. Any one of us who did get sent down; be it a short stretch or a longer one; they would be looked after on the inside and on the outside i.e. their family; wife and kids. We were not the only crew to abide by those sorts of rules almost every professional villain or gangster from the old school lived by that 'code of honour'. I am not trying to justify myself here and pretend I wasn't ruthless in some of the crimes I committed; it would be hypocritical of me to deny it.

I will give you a brief insight into how it was with us. First though I would like to point out that (and I am just speaking for myself here) when we were about to commit a robbery, especially if it was heavy; for instance steaming into a bank or some security depot, for me and some of those who were involved, it could be a nerve-wracking experience. It wasn't glamorous or anything like that, certainly not the way it is sometimes portrayed in the movies or on television.

I particularly remember one of the many armed robberies we

were involved in at that time; it was a security depot somewhere out of town. I was inside the premises armed with a sawn-off shotgun and two of my accomplices were attending to the main employee; who was according to reliable information, in charge of the goodies that we had come for. Another one of our team was sat-off outside waiting in a fast piece of transport whilst all this was taking place. As I mentioned before, it was all tense; our adrenaline was pumping away like mad, time and speed was of the essence; we knew through experience that we only had minutes to do this. I was holding and pointing the gun at five of the office staff, who were all facing me with their backs to a wall. For a brief minute or so an eerie silence descended, except for a distinct sound which was coming from a young woman standing holding a tray of cups and saucers in both hands. She was trembling with fright and the crockery she was carrying was rattling violently. I think she must have been the young office junior, and unfortunately for her she was caught up in it all. I could feel for her and what she was going through. We didn't come to harm anybody or shoot any of these people; I had stipulated this to them all at the beginning. The money we were robbing wasn't theirs. I could see the predicament this young girl was in; she was staring at the barrel of the gun. I lowered the gun, pointing it to the floor. There was an office table and a chair nearby. I pulled the chair away with one hand and said to her,

'Put that tray down love.' She nervously put the tray down on the table. I then beckoned to her to sit down, which she did. I then leaned over to her.

'I'm just as frightened as you are. Nobody is going to hurt you. You will be ok.' I quietly reassured her we would be gone in a couple of minutes.

Now because I showed a little bit of compassion to her, one of the office staff; a tall guy took it as a weakness and stepped forward. I immediately sprang into action and pointed the weapon at him.

'Don't be a silly bastard.' I shouted. 'Be sensible.' He backed up again and stood frozen to the wall.

What I can't understand about an incident like that, is how some idiots would literally risk their lives to save some rich fat cat's money. If those sorts of people want to be heroes, why don't they go and beat some lowlife muggers up who rob from old people?

Anyway, that's the way it was and that's the way we were. The old-style villain has long gone. It's the end of an era. What we have now is marauding criminals with no morals, dignity or loyalty. In the end, it was this lowlife that eventually got to me. This particular band of scum are the lowest breed of today's criminal, and I would class them as being as bad as paedophiles. Why? Because they would sell children to paedophiles if they could make money out of it. They prey on the ordinary man and woman on the street, as well as other criminals. They have no morals or scruples, they are known as 'hyenas' amongst the criminal fraternity in Liverpool.

Names; that is, the top well-known gangsters, mean nothing to them. It doesn't matter that the villains they take on have reputations as hard-cases, or have even killed in the past. They will still try to have them off.

This modern day gang of scumbags venture out at night like a gang of scavengers to carry out their so-called graft. Then they return to their dens of iniquity, knowing full well that they will be hard to find if you wanted to hunt them down. This new breed of lowlife believe they can't be hit back.

But they can.

I know because I did.

FRIDAY, 30 OCTOBER 1998

On this date I was found not guilty of a contract killing and walked out of Liverpool Crown Court a free man. I had been accused of pumping three bullets into the head of a notorious Liverpool villain, a member of a despised lowlife gang.

Just before leaving the court buildings, I was confronted by two detectives from the Liverpool Murder Squad, the very same who, only a few days earlier, had been swearing my life away, giving evidence against me. They told me they had reliable information that there was a contract out on me in connection with the case. I was going to be murdered, they said, and they asked me if I wanted police protection. My answer was 'No.' I knew that if somebody was determined to kill me, all the police protection in the world wouldn't help. I know, and so do the vast majority of other villains, that the police lack resources. They can only offer protection for a short while. Let's face it; in this day and age, the police, or bizzies as we call them, can't look after themselves, never mind the public.

Liverpool people have always called the police bizzies; they acquired that nickname years ago because we were all led to believe they were busy at their work. In my honest opinion, they don't deserve that title any more. They should all get off their arses and out of their cars they are always driving around in, and do a bit of walking for a change. Maybe then their name would revert back to the other nickname they had... plod; because that is what they used to do, plod up and down on the beat.

Even though I rejected their protection, it didn't mean I wasn't bothered by the threat, because I was. Who wouldn't be? Nobody is infallible and I never underestimate another person's capabilities. It doesn't necessarily have to be a professional contract killer who will shoot you. A lowlife drug addict can be approached more easily and much more cheaply. Show them a bag of gear and these dregs will have no qualms whatsoever about killing you. Their minds are so fucked up that they won't even think about the consequences. But the person who instigated the killing would have to be plain fuckin' stupid; how can they trust someone with a bad drug habit to keep their mouth shut? Especially when police can get hold of them, as they inevitably do. Put any addict under pressure from the murder squad and they will just roll over. There are some villains who just don't think or apply any common sense before they act. Then there are others who have no self-control, or who think they are untouchable.

Take the Krays. In the past, they killed men in front of witnesses. I know the men they killed might have been scumbags and bullies, but to kill in front of witnesses just takes the cake. You always have to consider the aftermath. I know, I've been there. In the past I have been grilled by police on many occasions over shootings and murders, but have always venomously denied these accusations and charges. As I've said before, I was innocent of everything of which I was accused.

After my brief encounter with the Liverpool Murder Squad, I left that Crown Court freely, my first independent act for twelve months... but those words still rang in my ears; 'There's a contract out on you.'

When I was released I was dead chuffed to have all my staunch supporters waiting for me. Good people, good men, who possess dignity and respect. This takes me back to when this notorious murder trial was at its height. I will never forget what my family and friends did for me, particularly my brothers, who had huge placards made with slogans written on them, strongly stating how unfair the case against me was being handled by the police. Every time I made an appearance at the Liverpool magistrates' court, the place was always fully packed tight and those friends of mine who did not gain entry would take it upon themselves to parade up and down outside the court in Dale Street, strongly protesting, carrying their placards. And that was all done during the bitter cold weather in the depths of winter.

I remember there was a time I was being escorted from the back of the court buildings and I could hear car horns blaring like mad as people drove past supporting all the people marching. Mind you, that is just typical of good Liverpool people. I would like to thank all those staunch friends who were there for me; big Tony Kermo, John Kirkby, (Broadhurst) Tony Woods, Evo, and all the rest, there are too many names to mention, but I know who you all are and will always be grateful for all your loyal support. Big Martin was there beaming, along with all the rest of the boys, and our Jimmy and Joe; my two brothers, and the rest of my loyal family were all there to greet me as well. I will never forget what my family and friends did for me, especially in the build up to my trial.

Moments after receiving my brilliant result (a not guilty verdict) my mind and body began to return to normality; the tension and anticipation of the arduous trial was washing away. I felt so good especially being surrounded by these loyal friends and family of mine, but then my adulation was briefly interrupted. I had glanced around the court whilst all this merriment had been going on and I had caught sight of two men sitting at the back of the crowd. They couldn't seem to help betraying their true feelings of disappointment at me being set free. Their faces were full of spite and hatred. I had recognised them in the crowd at my trial on more than one occasion, sitting in that court like vultures awaiting my conviction and imprisonment, hoping I would be sent down to do a life sentence. They know I know who they are; two old enemies from my home area of Huyton, Liverpool 14. All I can say is, if you two dogs ever read this book, as you no doubt will, I'm sorry to have disappointed you both.

The press and television were there as well, hungry for photos and statements. On the steps of the courthouse moments after my acquittal, one of the journalists said to me that of course I was guilty so, 'Give us the exclusive story and you can have a nice few grand.' He went on to say how I had nothing to lose since I couldn't be retried for the same crime. I couldn't believe the barefaced audacity of this man, in front of all my family. I told him, as politely as I could in that situation to 'Do one!'

As this pantomime was drawing to a close, one of my brothers got me to his car and sped us away, closely followed by the rest of my family. All I wanted in the world at that moment was a shower, some fresh clothes and just to chill out. There is nothing in the world like coming home after being inside, especially having resided at Her Majesty's pleasure in the Category A prison of Strangeways, Manchester.

As the car drove me further and further away from those

memories, I remember thinking of how I'd been caged up for a year awaiting my trial. I was found not guilty by a good, honest Liverpool jury and what did the court officials and the judge do? Fuck all! Nothing. Not one word of apology. Not one ounce of consideration for the misery my family had suffered. I truly think it's because they still believed I was guilty, and I know for a fact that most of the Liverpool Murder Squad do. I just let my eyes close and thought about all the people who had spent a year waiting for me to trip up, willing me to fall. I knew that none of them could touch me, and as we approached my house, I was still wrapped up in these thoughts. Home... I couldn't wait to get inside and close the door on all that had gone on.

CHAPTER 2

I live in a fairly good suburban area of Liverpool called West Derby. The centre of West Derby is a quaint little village adjacent to Croxteth Park, home to the magnificent mansion that was once the residence of Lord Sefton. He bequeathed the park and the land to the local people some time ago. The history of this part of Liverpool is extraordinary. Lord Sefton's ancestors were of French origin; Molyneaux, and their family tree can be traced back to Norman times. The village itself is still home to the original coach house, courthouse, village stocks and the pub; The Sefton Arms, the tenancy of which belongs to great friends of mine. They serve excellent food and give great service. I often visit the place. It is also recorded that Oliver Cromwell marched through the village during the Civil War. Liverpool, like any city, has its rough and deprived parts but many people are unaware of how beautiful much of the city and its surrounding areas are. All true Scousers love the city... and I am no exception.

Thinking about this made me forget the trial as we passed each landmark on my journey back home. When my brother stopped the car outside my house, he switched off the engine. But as he turned to me, I could read on his face that something was wrong, something he'd not mentioned at the Crown Court. His face was full of worry, but I was home and I got out of the car.

'What's wrong?' I asked, heading for the front door.

I knew I should wait but I had been thinking about this moment for a long time.

'Charlie.' This time my brother's voice stopped me. 'Before you go inside, you'd better get yourself ready for a shock. It's been vandalised inside-out. The bizzies have gone to town on everything and smashed the house up.'

I opened the door, not sure how to respond. I couldn't believe it. My dreams of a peaceful return to the comfort of my own home were shattered. It was a scene of total devastation; some jealous bastards had been on a frenzied rampage. Everything was damaged or destroyed. I walked slowly through the debris that had been my home and as I went, I just saw more and more of the same.

Upstairs, my daughter's bedroom floor had been ransacked. Her pride and joy, an expensive collection of dolls, had been decimated. Dozens of little porcelain bodies had been decapitated and their crushed white heads that she had dressed and loved lay at my feet.

My head was done in. My own bedroom was even worse. Wardrobe doors had been torn off their hinges and long splinters from them were strewn around. Sleeves were torn from all my suits; every item of clothing had been turned to rags. The glass top to my dressing table was broken into bits. I couldn't believe it. There was no need for this fuckin' carry-on.

Going downstairs, I found that not one part of the house had escaped them. The spacious lounge had once boasted beautiful moulded plasterwork on its high ceilings, but for some inexplicable reason it had been broken off. It lay in pieces all over the carpet. The large antique mantelpiece lay alongside of them, leaving a hole in the chimney-breast where it had been. The furniture had suffered the worst. My soft-hide three-piece suit had been worked over with a Stanley knife, leaving the stuffing spewing out of it. My beautiful gilt mirror, with matching goldframed chairs were all damaged beyond repair.

When I finally looked in the back garden, it was like Beirut; an absolute war zone. The swimming pool, surrounding patio and rockery were totally demolished. I was dead sick to discover that all the shrubs and trees that I had hand-planted years ago had been torn out and lay broken on the rubble. These beautiful trees and shrubbery had ensured my privacy and seclusion as well as providing a good habitat for the birds. Before being stuck away in the nick, I had enjoyed pointing out the different species of birds and their nests to my daughter. Out of the fifty trees I had planted, only seven remained. The rest had been chopped down at the hands of those fuckin' butchers. With the trees gone, this site could be seen by anyone; the humiliation and devastation was on display to my neighbours, something these snide bizzies had certainly intended.

The police had clearly been so vindictive towards me over the murder I'd been charged with because there was absolutely nothing to substantiate their allegations. So they resorted to this mindless vandalism against my property. All the damage had taken place while I'd been in custody and the police had been the sole occupants of the house. Not even my own family members had been allowed on the premises. This destruction was the result of a so-called 'lawful search' stretching from November 1997 to early 1998.

I hate vandals; I always have done. When my brothers and I were kids, we never dreamed of breaking and destroying things just for the sake of it. I have always appreciated and respected the good things in life that are there for our use and enjoyment. This is down to the way my parents brought me up.

These days, vandalism is out of control; not a day goes by without bus shelters being smashed, lovely parks and gardens being destroyed and even fire engines or ambulances being stoned. The sickest and most inexcusable of all acts of vandalism is the desecration of graves. Imagine people going to visit their loved one's grave only to find it defaced and smashed at the hands of a vandal. What is wrong with the scum who do this? There's no difference between them and what these so-called policemen did to my home. They were on a rampage like any other beast on the street. In my opinion, they are no better than the mindless, destructive thugs of today. The damage caused to my home was estimated at £63,000.

Shortly after being released, I took legal advice and, with the strong evidence we had against them; they were caught on video camera by one of my good neighbours, carrying out their destruction, we took the case to be heard at the High Court. I knew what the outcome would be and so did they. At this point, their legal team made me the paltry offer of £10,000. This wouldn't even compensate for the ruined carpets and curtains. Cheeky bastards; as far as I was concerned they could all go and fuck themselves. I sat down with some of my family and we discussed how to make the place habitable again. With a lot of hard work, we turned that eyesore back into a home.

Something I have always valued, particularly in Liverpool, is how good people rally round in a crisis. I was genuinely surprised and touched when many of my neighbours called round to offer support, some of them even bringing congratulations cards and bottles of wine. Most have been supportive during my time inside, but for many of them it was a way of saying 'thank you' for things I had done for them in the past, particularly for the old-age pensioners.

Sense of community is something that is dying in many parts of Liverpool; and the rest of the country for that matter. Without knowledge of those around you and a readiness to help them in a crisis, the support available for many people is limited to a few friends and family. Particularly where bad crimes such as muggings and violence are concerned, this leaves many of them vulnerable, no one more so than the elderly. I have lost count of the number of conversations I have had with my elderly neighbours as they recount tales of fear and intimidation. Certain old ladies near me told me regularly that they couldn't sleep and felt totally unsafe in their homes. I could see they were reaching breaking point with the endless newspaper coverage of burglaries and violence in local areas.

I use the term 'burglary' with caution. No longer does it mean what it used to; breaking into some lord's mansion and having the silver, oil paintings and jewellery away. Good luck to anyone who has riches away from the well-off, I've got nothing against that where those who can afford it are concerned. After all, how did the rich get there in the first place? Burglary has now changed into a new form, lowlife scum targeting the vulnerable, the widows and the infirm. Many of the ladies I spoke to lost their husbands in WWII, a sacrifice made to secure a better and safer life for their wives and for generations to come. I would sit and listen to their stories for hours but many of them were too old to be living alone.

Despite everything though, they were proud, decent people holding onto their homes, their few belongings and their memories. When I found out that many of them weren't even eating decent hot meals in the winter time, I decided to do something myself.

Old Muriel lived next door, Mrs Binns was opposite and just around the corner was old Dolly and her friends. I used to make sure these poor old ladies got a good roast dinner from me every Sunday without fail. My daughter, who was only a little girl at the time, used to take the meals round to each and every one of them. It was no wonder they were as scared as they were. The world as they had known it no longer existed. They knew that it was only a matter of time before their homes suffered at the hands of the lowlife who were spreading terror like a disease throughout the neighbourhood. This scum didn't just rob; they seemed to enjoy ferociously beating these poor women and would hang around after the robbery to do it. These women knew this. Like me, they had seen the photographs in the newspapers of other old people, their faces black-and-blue after meeting one of these animals in the dark.

I know it might sound like I'm having a go at the police with regard to terrible events like this but, let's face it, they never seem to be around when something serious happens. Yet if some minor car accident occurs in the same proximity, like, for instance, a plastic bumper or a headlight gets broken, there'll be a swarm of bizzies in minutes. You can't help wondering if they've got their priorities right. And it's not only the police, but the courts and authorities, too, who support this attitude; that money and property, are valued more than the quality of people's lives.

Two mates of mine were good family men, good to their wives and kids, men of decency, who would go to the aid of an elderly person who may be getting mugged, or a woman about to be raped, men who wouldn't dream of doing any real harm to anyone. Yet just because there was a large amount of cash involved in the robbery they committed, of which they were found guilty at their trial in the Crown Court, a certain judge sentenced both of them to 20 years. It is not just their liberty that is taken away; as if that was not enough they're also deprived of their wives and children; who suffer badly, too. That same judge, in court the very next day, could be dishing out probation to a rapist or child molester. I will never be able to fathom out how this can be called justice.

After hearing and seeing the fear in the eyes of my elderly neighbours, I was sickened about it all, so I decided to act. Maybe it is called 'taking the law into your own hands' and, if that's the case, then so be it. Nothing was being done to help these poor old people; they had nobody else to turn to.

First, I went round to visit some of the pensioners in their homes, insisting they took my phone number, telling them:

'If you need me, ring me any time, day or night.'

Second, I fitted a few bolts and locks on their bedroom doors, although, believe me, I'm no DIY man! But it made them feel more secure, especially Old Muriel. After making sure those initial safety precautions were taken care of, a few days went by. Then the phone calls started in the middle of the night. Every night, these women suffered; every night they had no escape from the noises, real or imagined, unable to sleep. Sometimes they would ring at three or four in the morning but I kept my promise and always got up - half-asleep, the majority of the time. Usually, they were false alarms. It would be a cat knocking a milk bottle over, or just the wind. Nevertheless, I'd given my word so I always got up to investigate. This went on for several weeks, until Muriel rang and this time it was no false alarm.

My patience had paid off. It was 4.00am and the poor woman was out of her mind with fear; she could hardly speak. I could practically hear her quivering down the phone as she spoke. In a hoarse whisper she said, 'Charlie, I just heard my kitchen window being broken.'

'Calm down,' I told her. 'I'm on my way. Keep your bedroom door locked. I'll be right there.'

Jumping out of bed, I quickly pulled on my jeans. Just as I got to my kitchen door, I pulled a claw hammer out of my toolbox, sticking it inside my belt. I started opening my back door quietly; I crept up to the garden fence, determined to catch these scum bastards. Peering over the fence, I saw one of those young pricks halfway through Muriel's ground-floor window, while another one was keeping watch. I crept along the fence until I got to the lowest part, all the time keeping my eye on the one nearest to me. My face was dead close to the wood of the fence as I watched the two of them working their way into Old Muriel's house. One was at the window. He turned to his partner and gave him the nod.

Then he slyly grinned and it was then I completely lost it.

I jumped over the fence towards them and as soon as they saw me they tried to fuck off, but as they reached the bottom fence I was on them. I grabbed the nearest one by the coat and yanked him off the fence, pulling him back on top of me. We both hit the ground. As I pulled myself up, I saw that the little prick had pulled a blade on me.

'What the fuck are you going to do with that?'

He screamed at me, 'Get back... Don't come near me or I'll cut you to fuckin' bits...'

'Oh, will you now?' I said.

I was much quicker than him, and I just went berserk with the hammer. I couldn't stop myself, I started smashing his head and face in, taunting him for how 'hard' he was, terrorising an old woman. It only took a few minutes. His body was in a right mess.

The other one had got right off, so I left this dog on the floor and went to find Old Muriel to check if she was OK. I told her I had chased them away and not to worry, there was no way they were coming back. I also told her not to bother ringing the police and that I'd be round to fix the window in the morning. I then went back to find the scumbag I'd left down in the garden. He was lying on his back, moaning and, as I looked him over, I could see he was done right in where I had caved his head in with the hammer. I realised I'd probably gone too far. I started dragging him towards the front of the house. My intention was to leave him out on the road, away from both our houses. I propped him up, sitting against a wall opposite my house. He was going nowhere, and I left him, thinking he would pick himself up and take himself back to where he came from.

I went back to mine to wash and get back to bed. My bedroom was at the front of the house, and Joan; my partner at the time, was asleep, unaware of any of the events that had just taken place. After half-an-hour or so I took a look out of my bedroom window to check on him, but he was still lying there, propped against the wall in the position I'd left him in. It didn't look as though he'd even blinked in that time.

I started to get a bit worried, wondering if he was going to wake up at all. I tried to get some sleep and forget about it but after a further ten minutes I checked again and he was still there. By now I was convinced he was dead. I'd killed him! In my mind, I started planning how I was going to handle the situation. I thought, 'I've got to get him in the boot of my car and drive out to the country with a spade and bury him.' I knew if the bizzies ever found out I'd be back in that dock in no time. But as I watched, he slowly started to rise off the floor. It was like watching somebody coming back from the dead, as he dragged himself down the road and out of sight. I finally got back to bed and tried to sleep, thinking how easy it is to kill someone in a fight.

I do know that, after this incident, the old ladies living by me never got attacked or broken into again. Some months later, the police caught a scumbag in West Derby in the act of terrorising a woman. I believe he was the one responsible for all the other attacks and he was sentenced to 12 years. In my opinion, he should have been put down.

You, the reader, may think I was out of order for what I did to him. You might think it would have been better to have rung the police and let them deal with it. Maybe you're right, but look at the other side; what if this animal had made it into Muriel's house? Why was he carrying a knife to enter an old lady's home? Who knows what could have happened to her.

The reason I've described this seemingly small incident is because I have been portrayed by some people as a latter-day Robin Hood. Well, that is a load of bollocks.

Whenever my Firm committed some major robbery in the past, I certainly never went round giving away money to people. Sure, maybe a few quid went to family and friends, but definitely not to just any old Joe Bloggs on the street! What I *can* say is this: yes, I have taken the law into my own hands on many occasions throughout the years. For example: some of my friends and I have sat at the back of the Magistrates' or Crown Court and watched a child molester about to walk free because a loophole has been found in his case. I have been there and have heard the parents of the abused child shouting, screaming at the injustice, forced to watch as a judge lets one of these animals walk free. OK, we all know of these rare occasions when an innocent person has been wrongfully charged or accused, but when the evidence is so overwhelming against some of these evil bastards, and even when some of them have pleaded guilty, what punishment do the majority of them receive? Fuck all! So where is the justice?

I will now tell the truth and put the record straight about the rumours circulated about me over the years. Yes, I have nearly killed some of these 'beasts', as we call them, but I have only been one of many who've also handed out their own type of justice.

Several beasts passed through Walton Prison while I was working in the reception wing. This screw, who was married with kids of this own, hated them. He would always mark our card as to who was a beast. He would even show us what they had done to kids or women as the screws had all the records on them.

When we were told one had come in, these filthy beasts would have to have a bath before seeing the prison doctor. After going through this routine, they would be taken to the protection wing for their own safety. One of the screws would tell one of the reception lads which prisoner was a sex case, and then the screw would turn a blind eye while the attack took place. It usually happened in the bathhouse. I have seen some of the terrible hidings these beasts have received. And I have done some bad damage to them myself.

When we had been shown what they had done to those little kids, it turned your stomach. Some of the things they had done were beyond belief. You just couldn't imagine that grown men, if you can call them men, could do those filthy things to little children. It was no use the do-gooders on the outside saying these people couldn't help it, they were sick and various other excuses, all I can say to that is that those beasts know right from wrong.

One of the worst cases I knew of was when this cruel bastard had a little girl locked in a room all day and, when he returned home, he would go up to that kid's room and torture and abuse her. She was only five or six years old. Can you imagine that poor kid? To be left alone in that room; waiting for that beast to come home each night. The poor child died in the end. Yes, I nearly killed a few of those bastards who came in for child molesting or rape or whatever you want to call it. I don't regret one thing that my pals or I did to them.

The odd thing about some of these animals is that they can pull the wool over your eyes. I remember once this bloke had just come in. He had just been sentenced to six years. He was a smart-looking fella; he looked and acted like one of the boys. I got talking to him before he went through reception and he told me he was in for hijacking lorries. He seemed, as I thought, a nice enough fella. When his turn came to go through, the screw in charge called me to one side and told me this so-called lorry hijacker was in for abusing his own little daughter and son. I just couldn't believe it. I said to the screw,

'Are you sure? Has there been a mistake about this fella?'

He showed me his charge record which convinced me. A short time later, when he went for his bath, he got boiling water thrown over him, which was justified, as far as I was concerned.

I often witnessed these beasts on visits and their wives, who, you would think, would be the first ones to condemn them, actually coming to visit them. It makes you wonder what sort of mothers they are. I can't understand the authorities or the Government who seemed to be so lenient when it came to dishing out sentences to these perverts. It seemed to be another case of valuing money more than a child's life. I remember a prison doctor pulling me to one side in reception one night and saying to me,

'Seiga, don't hit any of these sex cases until after I have examined them. They are getting sent into me with black eyes and everything.'

And that was the attitude of the prison doctor!

I still stand my ground and believe that what I did was right. If certain people think I'm wrong for taking the law into my own hands, well, that's OK by me. But I wonder if these same people would change their minds if it happened to them, or if it was their own child being molested or their own grandparents being mugged.

CHAPTER 3

Waking up to find myself in my own bed, in my own home, was unbelievable. Until I opened my eyes, I'd thought I was having a lovely dream and that when I woke up I would find myself back in the same prison cell. My daughter's laughter floated up the stairs and I could hear a pleasant conversation taking place.

'Dad!' my daughter called, 'Are you awake? Your breakfast's almost ready!'

When I heard this, I knew I was at home. I could smell the food and, in no time, I was back at the kitchen table, surrounded by family and laughter, devouring a plate full of crispy bacon and fried eggs, washed down with a big mug of tea.

The world was once again beautiful. It's ironic; most of us don't appreciate the simple things in life, we take it all for granted. But when I was caged up in prison, facing a life sentence for murder, I made a vow. If I was found not guilty and freed, I would never complain or moan about anything ever again.

Just one hour later, I was moaning and screaming my head off. It turned out that in the twelve months I'd been away, my tank (money) had been heavily used. Obviously, if a pot is getting dipped into and nothing is being put back in, the money soon goes. Plus somebody I thought was a friend had ripped me off a fairly large amount of dough.

This was bad, but I knew there was still one thing I had left; my secret nest egg. Over the years, I'd collected a large amount of jewellery, gold, diamonds and such like. It was always meant to be something to fall back on, kept for that rainy day. Everybody in the business of crime has his or her own personal stash, just like those of big, wealthy businessmen when they cream off the top and defraud the taxman and the VAT.

Knowing I still had the nest egg softened the impact of the tank being bled dry. I had been a lot more careful securing the location of my long-term stash and so, feeling uncomfortable with this intrusion into my privacy, I went to check on it immediately. In my back garden was an old sandstone wall, completely covered with ivy. Only I was aware that one of the blocks was loose and could be removed. It was behind this block of sandstone, about a foot square in size, that the stainless-steel case containing my illgotten treasures was hidden.

I walked through the garden trying to ignore the devastation of my trees, plants and ornaments; that had still not been properly cleared and replaced, when I saw that the ivy was gone. My stomach turned as I walked ever more rapidly. The ivy had been completely cut away from the wall and I could see quite clearly that the very stone I was heading for was gone. Vanished. And so, too, of course, was my box. I was completely gutted; the dirty bastards had found my hiding place. Whoever cut that ivy away made off with about £350,000 worth of my jewellery!

But I couldn't report it, now could I, not when it had already been stolen in the first place? All villains know that a search of their homes by the police can uncover stashed readies or bent jewellery. The police know full well that the villains can't scream for it to be given back. When asked where it came from, they are only too glad to say it's not theirs and they've never seen it before. It's a 'finders-keepers' scenario.

Well, I was only two days out of the jug (prison) and completely wiped out... skint... penniless. At my age, approaching sixty, what the fuck can you do to earn wages? The days of a good robber (by that I mean armed blags, safe-breaking and such) have long gone. That all went in my youth, from the early 1960s to the late 1980s. Now we are left with thugs, rip-off scams and other types of slimy work associated with lowlife, and I refuse to have anything to do with that kind of graft. I remember someone once telling me, 'Principles won't feed you, Charlie.' But I would sooner have principles than be involved with that sort of backstabbing, dirty work.

Word soon got around about my predicament. This is the sort of situation where loyalties are tested and true friendship is proven. Some of the friends I expected to help, disappeared, and that I have never forgotten. Perhaps they thought I'd never get on my feet again. But if so, then they didn't know me well. I am a determined person, not one to be defeatist when things get rough. My pride and dignity would never allow me to lower myself to anybody, especially by asking for handouts. I will say, though, that my true loyal friends were there for me. I was never worried because I knew that if I had faith, old friendships would come through.

In no time at all, some of these men who had been well out of villainy for years, and were now well established legitimate businessmen, rallied round. My mate Gary, for instance, was a diamond. He came to see me and gave me a parcel of money, which contained a nice few grand; he bought me a decent car and he even took me on a boss holiday, with everything laid on for me in a beautiful villa with a swimming pool. Just what I needed to help me recuperate after being banged up in prison. Three other mates - Jimmy, Tony and Bill - also provided a massive support, and they helped me out enormously. It was unbelievable! A massive thanks to all of them, and of course to my family and so many others, who all helped me to pick myself up once I was out.

Despite the beautiful surroundings, the hot sun and people around me whom I loved, I still occasionally found my mind wandering, taking me back to prison. Nothing in the world will ever make me go back there, but having left, I find myself thinking of that place more often than I would like. Strangeways is not an easy place to forget, especially being on the Category A wing. It was there that I met a man who is without a doubt one of the vilest human beings I have ever met.

His name: Alan Lea.

Lea was being held in the punishment block when I first met him. His cell was situated directly below mine. Somehow, he found out who I was and, also being from Liverpool, introduced himself by shouting up at me through his cell window. It was always my golden rule to never talk to another prisoner through the cell windows, especially at this time, as my trial was so imminent. You never know who is listening, so I told him not to mention it.

There are certain prisoners who would willingly sell their souls testifying against you and giving false evidence, in return for a reduction in their own sentences. But most Scousers, when away from Liverpool, stick together and it was because of this that we struck up a bit of a friendship. To be honest, I felt sorry for him. After all, he was down the block, which is never easy, and he had nothing; no cigarettes, no phonecards, nothing. Phonecards are essential to a prisoner doing time; it helps alleviate the terrible anxiety and boredom if you can speak to friends and family.

I knew from first-hand experience what the hardships of life on the block, and worse, were like. When I first arrived at Leicester jail in the 1960s, I was met by a crowd of screws who were waiting for me. You would have thought I was a terrorist the way they treated me. I was taken to the punishment block straight away and told that if I caused any trouble, I would be sorted out. After a few days down the block I found out there was a convict there who worked as a cleaner and was known as a bully. I saw him throwing his weight around to a couple of the other cons. One morning, after I left my cell to 'slop out', he said to me,

'You are one of those Scouse bastards who think you're hard!' and he started to hurl abuse at me.

I saw the two screws watching and I knew it was a set-up. He was goading me into a fight and, as you can imagine, my temper got the better of me. I got stuck in and he was easy. As I fought him, he was screaming his head off and I knew what was corning next. The screws jumped me and although I was young and fit and could handle myself, I had no chance with all those bastards when they piled in on me. I was put in a strip cell in the hospital wing.

A strip cell was a degrading experience. You were stripped naked and the cell was completely bare. No bed, no chair, nothing! All I was given was a small sheet of canvas. Whenever the cell was unlocked, I was confronted by two screws. They brought my socalled dinner to me in a plastic bowl, which was kicked along the floor by one screw.

'Look, here's your dinner,' he was saying, 'eat it up.' As if I was a dog.

I picked up the dinner and threw it all over him. They both threatened me with violence while all I could do was stand in the corner and try to retain my dignity with the piece of canvas. It's funny, when you are in that position and especially when you are naked, you feel vulnerable and unready to fight. I just told them that the first one of them that came near me I would bite his fuckin' throat out, and although they would overpower me in the end, I'd get one of them. They just locked the door and fucked off.

What can you do? If you are being treated like an animal, you act like one.

So, knowing what he was going through, I felt for Lea, and when he asked for my help I gave it, making sure he was never without any of those essential little luxuries. At times, I even stuck my neck out for him, getting the goods smuggled down to him. I would have done the same for any young kid who was doing it the hard way down the block, as long as he wasn't a lowlife mugger or a sex case. So this was my relationship with Alan Lea.

It wasn't anything special; it wasn't even anything to talk about. But it was to this that my thoughts wandered back. Never really seeing him, speaking to him only rarely and thinking nothing of it. It was a tiny part of my prison world, but there it was. It was a friendship identical to dozens of others; a friendship that was becoming normality. Little did I know that, in reality, he was getting his claws into me.

After a few weeks, Alan was gone. He must have had a result in his own trial because the next time I saw him was when he walked into the Crown Court where my trial was being held. I remember that day vividly, sitting in the dock, surrounded by screws. Then I saw a figure in the gallery, grinning at me and waving like mad. I was up for murder and here was this scally waving like a lunatic.

To make matters worse, his appearance wasn't too impressive. He looked more like your typical thug and not someone I wanted the jury to associate with me.

'Who the fuck is that?' I wondered. 'Whoever he is, I can do without him.'

I had only seen his face briefly through my cell window, so it was only later that I realised it was Lea. Each day, as my trial progressed, Lea would show up and try to attract my attention. I assumed his intentions were good but it was reflecting badly on me and was a real distraction. I tried to ignore him, but these things don't go unnoticed by the judge, court officials, police or the jury. These people are always on the look-out to see who you acknowledge in the court. It makes sense to always be clean and well dressed. After all, I was fighting to protect the rest of my life; I was up on a murder charge!

Later, I had a visit from my two brothers and told them to have a word with Lea asking him to calm down and stop waving, or better still, to keep away while the trial was going on.

Lea must have taken notice because he never appeared in the courtroom again. He did, however, keep in touch with some of my family, especially one of my brothers, Joe. Our Joe remarked to me on one of his later visits that he thought Lea wasn't such a bad kid really, and seemed genuinely to want to help in some way; it's only with hindsight I can see how it was happening. This dog was still getting his claws into me and, when I think about it, I'm gutted at how gently and how effectively his crafty, cunning ways worked.

'Yeah,' I said to my brother Joe, 'I'm sure he's a good kid really.'

CHAPTER 4

After the trial as the weeks passed, I began to find normality again. I was seeing a lot of my family and as much as I could, of my daughter, Bridgett. I returned from the holiday with Gary a new man, recuperated and tanned and it was on this Thursday evening in November 1998 that I sat with a few members of my family around the dinner table. We had a good meal and were enjoying a good class of wine, the usual chatter was flowing; as it does when my family get together. I contemplated how much I missed this; Bridgett had grown up a lot in a year and I missed every lost second of it. She had blossomed into a lovely young lady of twenty and I watched as she laughed with her cousin Joan across the table from me. It gave me a warm feeling to see her happy again. She had endured so much during my incarceration and the build-up to my trial. It upset me when I thought of all the worry she had been put through.

Even though it had been hard for her, her support for her dad was dead strong. When I was arrested for murder, she had just finished her gap year before studying Law at university. She was loyal, she took a further 12 months out of her course; despite the effect this had on her studies. I know she is an extremely intelligent young woman, but I still don't know where she found the strength to cope with the ordeal.

All through her childhood she had believed me to be an ordinary businessman; I never revealed any of my past exploits. She didn't know what I had done, or who I had been. I was just Dad, which is why it's so amazing that when the truth did come out about me being a villain, she proved dead loyal. Maybe it was because I played such a strong role in her upbringing.

When her mother and I decided to part she was twelve and it

was agreed among the three of us that she should stay with me. My other children were a lot older than Bridgett and had long gone their separate ways. Like any parent, I found it difficult at times. It's never easy looking after a teenage daughter; trying to guide and nurture, but nothing compares with the feeling of pride you get when you see the adult they have become, as any parent will know.

I just wanted her to have a normal childhood and to appreciate the simple, nice things in life; to have good manners and, above all, not to be selfish or spoiled. In fact, I gave her all the traditional family values and respect that had been instilled into me by my mother. Of course, I wanted only the best for her; what parent doesn't? But, mostly, I wanted normality in her upbringing. And, I'll be honest, it was hard at times, but somehow I managed.

One thing I never envisaged was that I'd end up paying thousands of pounds for a private education for her, but, as it turned out, I had no choice. Seeing her achieve the best possible education was my top priority, so, naturally, I was concerned when I found out about problems she had so early on in school.

As a child, Bridgett attended the state-run junior school in West Derby, like thousands of other children before her. It was a beautiful little school; most of the teachers there were of the traditional type with old-fashioned ways and impeccable manners. All the kids who went there seemed respectful, wellmannered and happy. When my daughter was attending, she used to come running out to me at home time with a big, cheery smile on her face. All the other children were exactly the same. They were so happy there and I was satisfied that it was a good school, the perfect start to her learning.

As the end of her time there approached, she started getting really excited about attending senior school, just as most kids do. But only a few days after she'd started, I went to pick her up in the car and couldn't believe the change in her. Instead of greeting me in her usual carefree manner, she was withdrawn and sullen. As a parent, it's easy to tell when something is wrong and something clearly was. Finally, I got her to tell me why she was so upset.

'Dad, I'm going to have to start smoking and swearing!'

Don't forget, she was just eleven years old at the time. It turned out that the older pupils of fourteen and fifteen had been forcing the younger gullible kids to smoke, swear and God knows what else. When I heard this, I went mad. To think someone was trying to corrupt my young, innocent daughter! I told Bridgett to try to avoid them and, if it got any worse, then I would sort it out. Of course, it didn't stop, but I wanted her to deal with her first real tests in life on her own.

But then a few days later something happened that really did my head in. Her mother had gone to pick her up from school and when she finally came out she was sobbing her little heart out. When I got home from work I learned that a teacher had asked kids if any of them knew any songs or poetry. Those who did were told to put up their hands and wait to be asked to recite their piece. Those who did this would be allowed out of class first. My daughter was always brimming with confidence so she volunteered and put up her hand. She started reciting a poem to the class, something her mother and I helped her to learn, but when she was halfway through it this teach said.

'Sit down, Bridgett; you talk far too posh for this class.'

When I heard this, I went mad. The next morning, I told her mother I would take her to school; where I had an argument with the teacher and decided to put my daughter into private education. I never wanted any of this. All I wanted was what was best for my child's education. I knew that if I left her at this rundown school, even a bright kid like her would have ended up with no qualifications. She could have turned out like so many kids today - unruly, bad-mannered and bumming around on the streets taking drugs. I wasn't going to take that chance; I just felt sorry for the other 20 or so I had to leave there. I don't condemn all these council-run schools, and neither do I blame all state teachers. But it's a fact that the school my daughter was attending, and the class she was in, was crap as far as I was concerned. Besides, you only get what you pay for and what I eventually paid out for her education was

'It was that young kid I was telling you about, he was in Manchester prison with me. He was having it dead hard in there, always down the block; you know; the punishment cells. I felt dead sorry for him, the poor kid had nothing down there; no smokes, phonecards, he didn't even get any visits from anyone.'

'I suppose being the way you are; you took care of him didn't you?'

'Yes I did; it's hard being banged up in solitary, it was sad really, but you know what Scousers are like away from Liverpool in an out of town jail. They usually stick together.'

'Is he ok now?'

'Yes, he seems to be doing ok for himself, I think he's into the other gear [drugs]. I just hope he hasn't been followed here by any of the drug squad. I can do without all that lark. You all know how easy it is to get fitted up by the bizzies.'

'Those little scallies can bring it on-top for us.' Jimmy said. 'He should have got a message to you instead of just calling round to the house like that.'

'Alright Jim, I'm not into drugs, never have been, the bizzies know that and so does everyone else in this city. I'm dead against that shit that they peddle out to the kids!'

My other brother Ged interrupted.

'You can't be too careful, you know what some of those druggies are like, they can't be trusted.'

'Ok let's drop it now, the kid came round with good intentions that's all. I most probably won't see him again, you know what these young kids are like; they can't get up early in the morning, they're nocturnal; sleep all day and come out at night.'

Ged stood up and started to yawn and stretch, 'I'm doing one... are you two coming or what?' He was referring to Jimmy and Joe my other brothers who were sitting with us.

Joe got up stretching and said, 'I feel a bit done in myself, I'll have to get my head down, I've got to be up early tomorrow morning. I'm going hunting with my birds.'

Chris, one of my loyal friends who was also sitting in our company quizzed Joe:

'What do you mean hunting with birds? What birds?'

'Haven't you ever heard of falcons?' Joe replied. 'You know... hawks?'

'Oh those birds; I thought you meant the ones that wear skirts!' Chris replied laughing.

'You're fuckin' thick, Chris.' Joe said, turning round.

'Hey at least the ones without the skirts on can't fly away from you!' He retorted.

Everybody laughed at this, but Joe was serious when he replied,

'I'll never lose one of my birds. It's impossible; when I go hunting they are all fitted with a tracking device.'

It was time for everyone to turn in. We all said our usual good-byes, and my family and friends left for their homes and their beds. Only Bridgett and I were left. So, after saying goodnight we both went off to *our* beds too. Little did I know how valuable those precious few hours of sleep would be to me the next day!

CHAPTER 5

I was up bright and early the next morning ready for my shopping spree in Manchester. Bridgett was already awake and I could hear her rummaging around in her bedroom. I had already told her what our plans for the day were; a day devoted to her; where she could choose clothes, perfume and anything else she wanted, as well as even deciding which restaurant we would eat in. She could do whatever she wanted.

I'd been waiting to treat her like this since I got out of the other yard (prison) and Bridgett was made up at the idea.

We had decided to take the train to Manchester, as it's much easier than driving. Besides, train journeys are more relaxing and much quicker. The station was relatively close to my house, so we could walk there easily. It was about 8.30am and we were planning to catch the 9.00am train. Everything was set, except Bridgett; who was still dilly-dallying around getting ready. I shouted to her to hurry up.

'I'll be ready in a few minutes, Dad!' was the reply.

Just then I heard a car engine and a horn beeping outside the house. Looking through my bedroom window, I saw a Rover car in my driveway, the driver of which I couldn't make out. I knocked on the window, the car door opened and the driver climbed out. It was Lea.

He had kept his promise and had returned, and was now gesticulating wildly and pointing towards the car. To be honest, I had completely forgotten he had said he would come back this morning and I couldn't believe he was there as early as he was. For a scally like him to be up so early takes some doing, and at the time I gave him credit for it. I had the idea he must have really wanted me to have that car.

I shouted to him from the window that I would be down in a minute. I was also worried that he could make us late so I stuck my head around Bridgett's bedroom door and told her we would catch the 10.00am train instead. This would give Bridgett plenty of time to get herself ready and me more time to get rid of Lea. But Bridgett was nearly ready and could tell something was going on, so I told her about Lea and the car. She was not happy about the delay.

'Look, that car he's giving me has to be worth a few grand.' I said. 'One hour won't make much difference.'

She wasn't convinced.

'I'll buy you a Gucci or Prada dress instead of that Next clobber you were going to get!'

This did the trick. Kids love the designer gear, and I was always impulsive with money when I had it.

When I opened the front door, the first words out of Lea's mouth were,

'All right, mate, let's go and have some breakfast, I'm starving!'

I had already eaten, but I agreed; on the condition that we wouldn't be too long. I told him I had plans and had to be back within an hour. I got into the car completely unaware of what my fate would be. Suddenly, the front door to my house flew open.

'Dad! How long are you going to be?' my daughter shouted angrily.

I turned to Lea and he just sort of smiled and shrugged. I told Bridgett we'd be about three-quarters-of-an-hour.

As we started pulling off the driveway, Lea turned to me and said, 'Where to then, Charl?'

I suggested trying some of the cafes further down the main road, towards the city.

'I'll leave it up to you, then.'

He was actually making it my decision to go in that direction. So of course, when, after a couple of minutes, he said completely out of the blue, that his sister lived on that same route and would I mind dropping in on her to pick up the car documents and say hello, I agreed without really thinking about it. Anything, I thought, to pass the time and get back to Bridgett.

The buildings we were passing had made me think of the day I was acquitted, leaving the court with Jimmy. I thought about the nick and about the kind of con Lea had been, on his own and with no one. Remembering these things must have justified to me the gratitude he seemed to be paying me.

'It'll only take a minute,' Lea said excitedly.

'OK,' I said, letting him do whatever he wanted in order to feel better.

Within minutes, we were pulling up outside a rundown council house in Wavertree. I noticed the front door was already open, but thought nothing of it. That was nothing unusual round there, though I wasn't relishing the idea of going in. It looked a bit too scruffy for me.

Lea got out of the car and walked towards the house. I stayed put and watched the early morning bustle on the street. There were two men a couple of doors away, carrying a rolled-up carpet into a house. Their van was parked just a few yards away from where we had pulled up. I glanced up; a few women were passing the car and heading for the local shops with their bags and shopping trolleys.

Lea still hadn't come back and so I started looking the car over properly. It looked new enough, though not 100 per cent. But so what? I thought. With the papers I could sell it dead easy and make a nice few quid. Lea still hadn't appeared so I began to think about the day ahead, planning the walk Bridgett and I would take around Manchester. I couldn't afford to be too late or she would be really mad. She was dead excited about this little excursion, and if I was late she would make my life a misery going round those shops. I laughed to myself at the thought of it.

Just then, Lea appeared in the doorway of the house, holding a mug of tea. He beckoned me to come in, using the same wild arm movements he had made from the driveway half-an-hour before.

'Hey, Charl!' he shouted. 'We might as well have a quick cuppa before we get off. My sister is dying to meet you.'

I was reluctant to go in. For one thing; I thought maybe his sister would still be in her nightie, you know how some women are in the morning, and that would have embarrassed me. Also, to be honest, I didn't fancy drinking a cup of tea in that house; it looked far from being a clean home and I am particular in that way. It then occurred to me that Lea's sister might be the chatty type and keep me talking for hours. After all, it took him ten minutes to get back out to talk to me. I wondered how long it would take to get to one of the cafes down the road, to get parked up and then get served.

I opened the car door. I was sure it wouldn't take long to get the papers and I didn't want him or his sister to think I had no manners. After all, what was the worst that could happen?

I walked up the path and with each step I couldn't shake the feeling that somehow I knew I would be dead late now meeting my daughter. In just a few steps I reached the door and had my hand on the handle. I thought of his sister in her nightie with a cold mug of tea for me in her scruffy little house. I'm going to regret this, I said to myself. Then I walked through the door.

There are moments in my life, that when I think back to them, are like crossroads. Times when, although I didn't know it, I made a significant decision that was disguised as a small one. There's always one second that stays with you; when you know that at that one moment you still could have turned around and walked away. The point of no return, as they say. Like when a few of us, all those years ago, would get ready to steam in on an armed raid only to find out it had been a set-up.

Well, this has to be one of those momentous turning points. The colour of that door, the blemishes in the paintwork, the way I was standing, the clothes I was wearing, the smell of the house creeping out and the sound of the carpet-fitters in the distance; that entire moment is frozen in time and burned onto my memory. I was bracing myself for what I thought was the worst, but as that door opened and I stepped inside, that part of the world became hell. That was the instant at which my nightmare began...

The minute I walked through the door, it slammed behind me and the hallway collapsed on top of me. A gang of bodies that had been shadows a minute before were suddenly all round me and all I could hear was voices. Dead quick, the door was locked and a big juiced-up black guy, well over six foot, and only in his early twenties by the look of him, was standing in front of me holding a shotgun directly at my face and grinning like a maniac.

My mind was a blur, I heard a voice from somewhere say,

'You was the one who killed our mate. You're going nofuckin'-where...'

The shotgun came crashing down on my head. I was caught completely off-guard and went down straight away, not knocked out; but unbalanced. I looked up to see four of them surrounding me.

One of them was masked; wearing a full-faced balaclava. Lea stood over me with a sneer on his face. I started to gather my senses.

'You dirty, slimy traitor,' I said, 'what's all this about, you fuckin' dog?'

'We know you got a hundred grand for shooting the other fella. We want a hundred grand from your brother Joey. We know he's got plenty. I'm fuckin' warning you. You had better get it for us. If he doesn't cough up you're getting it right in the fuckin' head!'

Suddenly, things were falling into place; Lea, the car, the trial, his conversations with Joe, my brother. Even right back to when we were in prison. I thought, What a mug I've been, falling for this. Who did these pricks think they were?

'You won't get a hundred *pennies* from me!' I shouted from the floor. 'You can all go and fuck yourselves!'

Lea started screaming and then shouted to the rest of them. 'Do the bastard in!'

I should have been more tactful. If I hadn't betrayed my feelings to them, maybe they wouldn't have gone off their heads with me. The working-over I got was done real good style. They pounced on me like a pack of wild dogs. I had no chance; they were all young men in their twenties and I was approaching sixty. The big black fella caved my ribcage in with the butt of the shotgun and Lea produced some industrial tape which he started to wrap tight around my wrists whilst screaming his head off. By then, I was lying face-down, trying my best to shield myself from the blows. The one wearing the mask bent down and pulled a knife on me. He jabbed it into the side of my left eyelid and then held it against my face, shouting,

'I'm going to cut your fuckin' eyes out!'

I twisted away from the blade but he grabbed my head and started to smash my face in with the handle.

There were eight hands on me, inflicting as much pain as they could, and all of them were screaming to one another at the same time. I couldn't say how long it actually lasted, but it seemed to go on forever before they stopped. As they climbed off me, I could hardly breathe; my chest was pressed hard against my lungs and felt caved in by the blows inflicted by the big, black fella. My head was cut open and throbbing and the blood from this open wound was running down my face. With difficulty, I glanced up to see if I was about to get another working-over and I saw my own blood splashed up the walls. Letting go again, my face fell into the pool beneath my head. The smell of my own blood was dead weird. I was really done in.

Lea bent down to me once again and as calm as anything said that he wanted me to ring my brother Joe. He said to tell him to give them a hundred grand or I was going to get it. I just lay there in silence, waiting to find the strength to twist my head round and reply. Slowly, I raised my head from the floor and I saw the black fella with the shotgun cradled in his arms; he was looking down at me laughing.

'You're not the big licks now are ya?' He sniggered.

I shouted to them, 'Go and fuck yourselves, you rats!'

Lea went off his head. He started kicking my face in and then they all started working me over again. The black fella ripped off my shirt and started biting into my back, laughing hysterically, trying to tear chunks out of me as though he was a mad dog. I just couldn't defend myself with my hands tied. I have no idea how long this went on for, or how conscious I was throughout it, but eventually they stopped. I was still face down on the floor. Again, it all went silent before Lea told me to make the phone call.

I just stayed quiet. I refused even to speak. Apart from anything else, the way I was feeling, I was in no fit state to talk to anybody. Lea looked at me as he crouched next to my head.

'Are you going to do it? You fuckin' will when you see what I'm going to do.'

Then he shouted to one of them,

'Get that fuckin' kettle on, I'm going to burn his dick off. He'll soon open up.' At that moment, I realised how evil this snake really was. He was getting a kick out of all of this, a real lunatic and cunning with it. But my mind wouldn't stay straight. Flashes of the prison where I met this animal came into my mind. Memories of good people I'd used to smuggle stuff to this fuckin' dog, at great personal risk. As well as this, I kept thinking of my daughter, waiting for me, watching the clock. I was still cursing myself for letting this little prick lure me here at all.

One of them was standing over me with a full, steaming kettle of boiling water. When I saw they meant what they were going to do, I just went mad. I was already in terrible pain when they jumped me for a third time, but somehow; I don't know where I got the strength from, both of my hands were gripping tight hold of the old dirty loose carpet underneath me. I managed to prevent them from turning me on to my back. But now I was fighting for my manhood!

I struggled on the floor, Lea screaming the whole time, 'Turn him over. Drag his fuckin' pants down!'

Despite my efforts, they managed to pull my trousers down from my back, but still couldn't roll me over. In all the panic and confusion, Lea lost his head and threw the scalding hot water over the tops of my legs and the lower parts of my arse.

It's impossible to describe properly the pain that caused. Everybody knows what it's like burning themselves, so imagine that ten times worse over a skin area as big as your legs. I screamed in pain, but that animal was determined to empty the kettle on me. My skin fizzed and bubbled long after he had run out of water and the pain seemed to be worsening. I was losing consciousness but continued screaming, calling them every name under the sun.

Lea started to laugh and shouted to me, 'How do ya like that eh? You're not a big fuck-off gangster now are ya?'

I writhed there on the floor, the rest of them standing over me watching, until the black fella said, 'Give him the needle, Brian, that'll shut him up.'

He was speaking to Brian Airey, who turned out to be the owner of the flat and the one who had brought Lea the water. He was a physical wreck of a man, barely nine stone. His skin looked like it would drop off if you touched it. He disappeared, and I realised he was serious; I believed he was fetching me a needle for heroin. Once I thought they were planning on plugging me with heroin, I froze, partly at the thought of the heroin, but also because the burns were becoming excruciating. I twisted my neck round to look at the back of my legs. I couldn't believe what I saw. My skin was red raw and was starting to come away in sheets. I had never felt pain like it. I thanked God that the scalding water had never reached any of the vital parts of my anatomy.

A moment or two later my eyes were blurry and half closed due to the blood running into them from the wounds I had just received. I could see the thin and gaunt figure of Airey, with sunken eyes, slowly coming nearer to me. I opened my eyes wider and the picture of him became clearer. He had a silly smile on his drugged-up face and he spoke in a weird voice to one of the others.

'Hold his arm out for me.'

The smack-head had hold of a rubber tube in his mouth and a needle in his bony, filthy hand. He spoke in a soft voice to me, with a silly smile on his face.

'Charlie, come on Charlie, after you've been boxed you're gonna feel great.'

Trying to recoil away from him, I had regained my senses and I was panicking. I shouted, 'Don't put that filthy thing in me.'

The black fella had hold of my arm as Airey tied the tube around it and started pulling it tight, smiling. I could see he was going to shoot the dirty needle into my arm. Now I really started to panic. He brought the needle closer. I started struggling with what strength I had left, but the black fella held my arm tight.

The smack-head was smiling wider than ever now. I started shouting,

'Ok! Ok! Cut it out will you, I'll make the call. I'll make the call!'

Two of them dragged me up from the floor. My pants were still around my ankles. I could barely stand up. My back was throbbing from the blistering burns and cuts all over my body. I had finally given in to these beasts. Let's face it, who wouldn't?

I am certain that if I hadn't given in to them, they would have injected my body full of heroin and that was the one thing I couldn't handle. The thought of a dirty needle; which could be contaminated with AIDS, entering my body, made me more nauseous than the beating and scalding I'd already received. I had no choice and so I agreed to make the phone call.

They were dead convinced that Joe had plenty of money, which must have been a mistake made in one of the conversations Lea had had with my brother while I was inside. I was well aware how long Lea had been getting his claws into our Joe too. This copping for me had been planned for a long time.

They dragged me up off the filthy floor, and then took me to a room with heavy curtains over the windows. The room was dirty and empty save for a few chairs and a carpet covered with litter. Against a wall there was a dresser. I was forced to sit on one of the hard chairs, to which they taped my arms and legs. Try to imagine being strapped to a chair with your arse and legs scalded and blistering, the skin peeling off and the weeping sores sticking to the seat under you. Try and imagine your back burning where you've been bitten and torn. I was exhausted and fucked from the working over but I couldn't move because of the chair. I couldn't even see properly because of the blood running into my eyes from the cut in my head. I couldn't wipe it away; my own blood was blinding me!

These bastards wouldn't clean me up, give me any medication for the pain or cream for the burns. Not one of these animals showed any compassion. It was excruciating, but I was given no other option. After these dogs made sure I had no chance of moving, let alone escaping; Lea bent down to face me.

'We're going out for a short while,' he said. 'I'm warning you, don't try anything.'

As if I could, the condition I was in!

Brian Airey was left alone to guard me and Lea told him, 'Fuckin' shoot him if he tries anything.'

Airey positioned himself opposite me, cradling a loaded shotgun, which he pointed at my head. Lea said they were going to buy a new mobile phone. As they were about to leave, I called to Lea, asking him to untie my legs as the swelling from the burns was getting unbearable. I needed some medication badly; the pain was horrific. The scumbag just grinned.

'Do you think I'm fuckin' soft?' He turned to Airey. 'If he gets out of order, you know what to do. Shoot him.'

As they left, I just sat there thinking of every single little thing I'd done for him in prison, when he was crying that he had no one, that he had nothing. And this was the way he paid me back. I was still gutted at how I'd been deceived by this vile bastard. This lowlife reprobate had well and truly had me over. Now, when all I was asking for was some cold water to ease the pain of the burns inflicted by him, this dog showed no compassion for me at all.

Lea and the others were long gone and Airey and I were left alone. It was clear that he was the weakest link, the toe-rag in this pack of dogs. If I wanted to make it out of there alive, I knew it was him I had to concentrate on. Although my body was crippled, my wits were returning. In prison, as well as in the outside world, mental strength is as important as physical strength and there was an opportunity here to use some psychology. He was weak. At first, he looked dead nervous, sitting there with the gun pointing at me, totally silent. I knew that talking was the only way to make him relax, but I also knew I didn't have much time. There was no way of knowing how soon the others would be back.

Next to the shotgun, he had a cat lying in his lap, which he was stroking slowly and lovingly. Airey certainly seemed dead fond of that cat. I started talking to him, just testing him. I asked for some cold water, which he refused to give me, saying it was more than his life was worth if anything happened. I said to him, 'Take a look at the state I'm in, I can't even move my fingers. What's wrong with you?'

Eventually he relented and gave me a cold drink, holding the glass to my mouth. After sipping at the water I kept talking to him. I started wincing in pain trying to get my body comfortable.

'Can't you get something to cover me up?' I asked him.

My trousers were still down by my ankles and I knew that if they were to be pulled up it would make the pain worse as my skin was peeling away. He looked a bit nervous. He got up off his chair and reached for a jacket that was hung over the kitchen door. Showing me the jacket he asked, 'Is this ok?'

I nodded to him. 'Be careful!' I said.

He then placed the jacket over my waist and legs covering the private part of my anatomy. Sensing he was vulnerable I knew he was my only chance and I had to work on him fast.

'Thanks. Do you live here on your own?' I asked

'Now I do. My girlfriend used to live here but she's done one on me.'

'It's a bit sad that, are you gutted or what?' He started scratching his skinny arm.

'Yeah.'

Then after pausing he said, 'It's all down to the other gear, [heroin] anyway she fucked off.'

'Isn't there any way you can get her back?' I asked.

He started to shake his shaven head. 'Nah, she won't entertain me.'

'Why don't you come off it and get yourself clean?'

'It's dead hard, I've done the cold, and rattled a few times, but you know how it is, I end up back on it.'

By now I had got the animal more relaxed and I kept talking in a soft tone and sympathising with him. Getting closer and trying to win him over I asked him his name and he said his name was Brian.

'I heard the way Alan Lea was shouting at you earlier on.' I said. 'When we were both in prison I looked after him. I can't believe the way he has done this to me.'

'If I was you I would just get them the money,' he said to me. 'They're fuckin' psychos. Believe me; you will come unstuck if you don't.'

He started to relax a bit more and placed the gun by his side, still stroking the cat that he had on his knee. I started again to try and win him over.

'They've got you scared haven't they? I know he made you get the boiling water. It was all down to him, not you.'

'I just do what I am told.'

'If they *do* get the readies,' I said, '£100,000, you'll be ok then won't you?'

He answered me in a high pitched voice:

'You're fuckin' joking aren't ya? They're only giving me a grand.'

'That's bang out of order,' I said, making out I was sympathising with him.

We paused for a moment. I winced with the pain from my blistering body; it was excruciating. I caught Airey looking at me. He could see I was in agony. He put his head in his hands and then he shook his head at the thought of what I must be going through. I started to use my clever street instinct and began to speak to him slowly and deliberately.

'You have never really heard of me, have you?'

Shaking his head, he replied, 'No, I haven't.'

'I have plenty of strong backing and we have money, untie me and I promise you, you will be taken care of.' I paused for a moment. 'Come on, we can both get out of here.'

He started to look frightened and nervous.

'I can't, I can't. They'll fuckin' kill me!'

With that he walked over to a dresser, pulled open one of the drawers, and took out his drug taking accessories. I could plainly see it was a smack outfit.

He sat back on his chair and prepared his arm; tying a rubber tube around it and then pulling it tight with his teeth. This arm resembled a decaying piece of black and blue meat. The punctures in it were innumerable. He finally chose a vein and tapped it hard with his fingers. Then he pushed the filthy needle into his meatless limb. I watched this procedure taking place with disgust, and shudders overcame me. This loathsome creature sat there surrounded by the filth and squalor that he lived amongst. He finally sat back with a pathetic vacant look on his face. I knew he was really off his head. I just looked at him shaking my head and thinking, That's it, I've got no chance of getting out of this fuckin' hell hole now!

About ten or fifteen minutes later I could hear the noise of the front door being opened; the other scumbags were back. Lea came into the room first, followed closely by the big black fella. I never did see the fourth person's face; but there definitely were four of them. It crossed my mind that perhaps the fourth person knew me. Maybe he always kept in the background so I couldn't identify him. I am still puzzled; even to this day, I don't know who he was, but time will tell. I vowed there and then tied to that chair, that if I got out of there alive I would one day track down that mysterious character. In the end, I always do.

'Are you still fuckin' about with that stupid cat?' Lea snarled at Airey.

He tossed the phonecard towards him. 'Hurry up and get that sorted.'

Airey diligently began scratching the panel off the card. While this was going on, the black fella and Lea told me what I should say when I spoke to my brother. Lea stared at me then said coldly, 'I'm warning you... no fuckin' tricks or we'll put one right in your head.'

CHAPTER 6

Horrifically tortured with scolding hot water, beaten to fuck, and threatened with a bullet being pumped into my head if I didn't go along with these filthy scum bastards. I now had to talk to my brother in the state I was in. It was essential now that I played the game according to their rules... only for the time being. By doing it this way both my brother and I had a chance of seeing each other again and taking these fuckin' lowlife degenerates out!

The plan was for the black fella to hold the phone to my mouth while Lea had a shooter pressed to my head. Once again, they recited what I had to say to my brother. I had to tell him I had been copped for by the other crew. He would know that 'the other crew' meant friends of the man I was accused of shooting dead in the contract killing. My brother had to put up a hundred grand, otherwise, I was going to get it... I would be shot dead!

After this briefing was over, Lea turned to retrieve the phone from Airey, who had been busy tapping the pay-as-you-go code into the phone, or so they thought. What he had actually done by scratching too hard at the card, was erase the number from it; rendering it invalid and unusable. When Lea realised this, he went off his head. He picked up Airey's cat and, just as a rugby player kicks a ball, he booted that cat all over the place. It was screeching its head off. In the next instant, he pulled a blade on Airey and threatened to stab him in the head, all because he ruined a lousy ten pound phonecard. Airey broke down crying like a little kid, partly as a result of the threats from Lea, but also because his cat had been nearly kicked to death. The black fella stepped in and calmed everyone down, then Airey was sent to buy another phone card, and like the gofer he was, he just jumped straight to it.

What sort of lowlife are these people? I wondered. They

wouldn't know how to sort out any real straight graft. Then again, on second thoughts, I realised that they couldn't be all that stupid. After all, they had managed to trick me into this filthy lair.

Airey came back with a new phone card. He was out of breath. Lea came over to me with a different shooter in his hand, this time a revolver.

'Just take notice what I'm gonna to do.' He said as he opened the chamber and loaded the bullets into it.

Then he pressed the gun against the back of my head.

'I'm warning you, I'll put one in your head, so don't try and fuck anything up.'

The black fella dialled my brother's number and held the phone to my mouth. My brother Joe answered and I relayed the events to him, giving him the instructions about the money exactly as I'd been told. It was good to hear our kid's voice. He told me he needed time but that he had a few grand he could lay his hands on right away. I also had to stipulate that on no account must the bizzies be informed and that he would be contacted later with further instructions.

It broke my heart telling him these things but I knew he'd deal with it well, and he knew I would have done the same for him. The phone was then removed from my mouth and switched off. It seemed that the black fella had more brains than the rest of them; he appeared more careful and calculating. For one thing, he wore gloves at all times. He gave me the impression that he was a lot more streetwise than them; he knew where he was coming from all right.

When I had had that brief conversation with my brother, I was then made to phone my daughter. After all, she had been the last one to see me getting into Lea's car outside my house early that morning. It was now well into the afternoon and my daughter would be out of her mind worrying about why I had not returned home or called. They knew this too and were concerned about how she might react. So I made the phone call and tried to reassure her I was OK. It tore me apart to lie to her, especially when she was so upset about the day being ruined. I made an excuse that I was unavoidably held up somewhere and that I shouldn't be much longer. It wasn't easy sounding relaxed with a gun pressed against my head and my blistered legs causing agony with every movement.

After this was done, they all sort of chilled out and began rubbing their paws together with glee; like the rats they were.

It had been several hours since I'd been battered and tortured on the floor in the hall and strapped to the chair. The pain from my wounds, especially my legs, was excruciating. My head felt as if it was going to explode. I had no trousers on and, looking down, I could see my legs had swollen to twice their normal size. The skin was also seriously blistered and was peeling off me.

Despite being nearly sixty, I keep myself fit and strong, but deep down I knew the odds were against me surviving this. I needed medical attention and something for the pain, but the strength of my hatred for these bastards was what spurred me on. I was boiling with adrenalin and anger. Strangely enough, it was the black fella, who just hours before had been on my back trying to tear my flesh with his teeth, who was the first to show anything resembling compassion. As for why, I don't know. Maybe he had finally come down from his raving lunacy. Then again, he might just have been thinking about the ransom money.

He told Airey to untie my legs and get me some cold water. Perhaps it had crossed his mind that I might not make it through the night. Certainly, their main concern was to keep me alive long enough to get the ransom money, so this move probably had little to do with my welfare. These animals always wanted it both ways. It was obvious they were planning to kill me after the cash had been paid by my brother, but they also wanted to collect from the Firm who had put out the contract on me.

Airey brought cold water in a plastic bowl that he placed on the floor in front of me. By putting both my feet in the bowl of water, I hoped to alleviate the pain and lessen the swelling. It didn't. I was still in agony; especially the back of my legs where the seat edge of the hard chair pressed against my raw exposed flesh.

A few minutes passed and Lea and the black fella wanted to make contact again with my brother. It was the same routine as before, brave-arse Lea with the shooter at my head, the other holding the phone to my mouth. When our kid answered, I had to relay back to him where the pick-up point would be. Incredibly, they decided to choose a bus stop opposite a main police station of all places.

Here's the way the conversation went with my brother:

'Alright Joe, I have to make this brief; there's a gun pressed at my head did you get the reddies?'

'Yes, but at the moment I can only pull-up ten grand, I need more time to get the rest.'

'Ok kid, here's what you need to do: Go to the bus stop facing the main police station in Wavertree in half an hour's time. There will be a fella there in a blue hooded jacket; he will be holding a white sports bag with the word Liverpool printed on it, just give him the dough kid then wait for the next contact.'

'I got it, but I need to hear from you every hour so I know you're alright, otherwise we will be hunting those fuckin' dogs.'

After hearing this from my brother the phone was immediately switched off by the black fella.

How cunning was this... there was a method to their madness; directly at the back of the bus stop was a road where the black fella could park, silently observing everything taking place, as contact was made by the one who was to collect the money. That of course, was Airey the toe-rag. This was all discussed openly in front of me; but they were all starting to get a bit edgy and paranoid in anticipation of the drop. Lea was going on to them, suggesting what he thought would be the best way to do it.

'Let him be the bag-man,' he said, pointing to Airey. 'He can pick the dough up.'

At this Airey protested.

'Why do I 'ave to be the one who does the collecting? I'll be identified, it's not as if I can wear a ballie, especially in the day time, can I?'

'Listen you soft cunt, you won't be stickin' your fuckin' neck out, the other two will be a few yards away from ya, sittin'-off in the car. I'm stayin' ere with Charlie. Everythin' will be alright, so stop fuckin' panickin' will ya.'

The black fella then turned to Airey.

'We'll be clockin' ya all the time, nothin' is gonna go wrong for fuck's sake, what's the matter with ya?'

'This wasn't my part of the deal though was it?' replied Airey. 'You all know it's my house that's being used; if anything goes wrong it will all be down to me.'

None of them was entirely sure what might go down. After they had spent some time briefing each other the black fella and Airey left for the pick-up. This left me and that vile bastard Lea.

Shortly after they had left, Lea started to watch me. He then had the audacity to ask me how I was doing. I would never have disclosed how I felt to him; I was burning with hatred for this animal. The fire of my hatred was all that was keeping me going. He then started trying to butter me up, trying to start a conversation with me.

'Look, Charlie', he said, 'I know what you're thinking. I had no choice but to bring you here. This is all down to that black cunt. He's running the show, not me. He wanted to cop for your daughter, not you. But I talked him out of it. You don't know him; he's a right fuckin' lunatic.'

He revealed what the black fella was going to do to my daughter. He described it in such graphic, obscene detail that my stomach turned. What he told me was so filthy and depraved, so insanely sick, that I just can't put it down in words. Lea was on a roll all right and just wouldn't shut up.

'I am like the way you were, Charlie. I'd rather be doing a good blag than this sort of graft. I had a good one lined up, it was a big PO on Cannie Farm, but the black fella wouldn't do it. He's got no fuckin' arse, or the brains for that sort of graft. I didn't really want any part of copping for you Charlie... it was all the black fella's idea, not mine, I want you to know that.'

Lea continued to chatter on inanely, but as far as I was concerned, he was talking a load of crap. He was just trying to justify his position and excuse himself from the situation. This animal wouldn't be pulling the wool over my eyes again; far from it. The betrayal I had suffered at his hands could never be undone; whenever I looked at him all I saw were lies.

He kept chatting on and on. I interrupted him briefly, knowing I had to be cautious about how I spoke to this slimy snake to avoid betraying my true feelings. I was still thinking of how I could escape and didn't want to jeopardise my chances by getting in an argument with the prick. So when I did speak to him, I chose my words carefully.

'Look, son, it was a decent thing you did bringing me here instead of my daughter. I appreciate that and I want you to know I will never forget it.'

I wanted to relax him, make him feel forgiven so he would chill out. Also, the less of a threat I seemed, the more of a chance I had of having it away.

He nodded, a grateful look on his greasy face.

I was just about to work further on this psychological ploy when his mobile rang. I watched as he answered it and started to grin insanely, something he had done virtually non-stop since he picked me up at 8.30am that morning. The look on his face said it all. He shouted, 'Nice one!'

They were on their way back. Everything had gone to plan.

CHAPTER 7

They were back soon after that telephone call. The black fella was holding a small kid's satchel in his hands and Airey followed behind. They crowded round the case, congratulating one another, messing about as if there was no tomorrow, like vultures. One of them emptied the money on to the filthy carpet and Airey started grabbing at the notes, throwing them up in the air. My brother's money. It seemed as if it was raining cash. In fact, there was only ten grand in the parcel, so it seemed plain to me that they were not used to large sums of money. I had to sit there and watch them like that for half-an-hour or so, like scruffy kids, playing around and laughing with my family's money.

However, there was something they didn't know. Unknown to them, or me, my brother had planted a minute tracking device inside the briefcase. This device was the size of a small capsule and they had totally overlooked it. They were much too preoccupied with the money, never expecting something like that in a million years. The quick thinking of my brother Joe meant that there was still a way out, thought, of course, I didn't know it. All I could see were these fuckin' dogs throwing my brother's money around and laughing their heads off. The sight of it made me sick, money that belonged to my brother that he had earned to support his family, now having these greedy bastards' hands all over it.

Joe had been clever in the panic and confusion of my phone calls. He had kept a clear head and it meant I had a chance. Don't get me wrong, Joe was not some kind of whiz kid. He doesn't have special gadgets lying around the house. On the contrary, our Joe was an expert falconer. He was the youngest of my brothers and inherited my mother's looks and nature.

He preferred to live nearer the country and owned a cottage on the outskirts of Liverpool where he could raise and breed hunting birds, such as falcons and hawks. He also bred coursing dogs as well. He owned one of the fastest racing dogs in the world, a saluki, and was fascinated by the creatures, once telling me that a greyhound doesn't inherit its name from the colour grey, but from the word 'gaze' as they hunt predominantly by sight. Their manner of tipping their heads back is not to open the nostrils to scent but to look down their nose at the landscape, the best way to make use of their incredible eyesight.

Joe is an intelligent man, and I have always respected this in him. I know how much he admired this quality in his dogs and how he always tried to have vision in an emergency. He always had the know-how to get out of a situation in ways you and I would never think of. Joe had been a hunter for years; even as young men, me with my other brothers and pals would be out enjoying the high-life of the clubs and the women, but not our Joe. He was never happier than taking himself off to remote parts of the country, hunting and tracking with his birds. And just in case one of these birds went missing a little far from home, he would use a tracking device to retrieve them. Only this time, he had used his expertise not to track a bird, but to start tracking me; his brother, captured by these venomous dogs.

However, it didn't take long for the party to turn the other way. Fairly soon, all the laughter turned to argument; typical of these no-marks. It seemed that Lea and the black fella were getting the biggest cut of the reddies and Airey was being fucked.

He had no choice really they had him over and he just had to accept a grand.

Airey was upset, and the argument ended with Lea sorting him out by saying,

'Fuck off, Brian, you know your chop was a bag of sand...' (a grand).

The black fella kept quiet, and just sat looking at me. He knew I was watching them for any signs of weakness and this was one. It was bad enough that they were fighting amongst themselves, but they were doing it in front of me. He knew quite well what I was thinking and he was dead right. Fuckin' no-marks. But Lea was up now and was on one. He shouted to the black fella,

'Are we going out then or what? This place is doing my fuckin' head in.'

Then with that he steamed out of the room. The black fella went with him after telling Airey it was the same dance as before; if I tried anything, shoot me! The fourth dog was still nowhere to be seen. It is possible he was listening from another room, especially since the argument didn't sound as if it was about a three-way split.

In a moment, they were gone and I was once again alone with Airey. This was the perfect opportunity, especially when he was really gutted with the others. He also hadn't told them what I had said to him about me getting away and protecting him; which was definitely a good sign. Before I said a word, Airey began to pour his heart out. Well, maybe I should rephrase that, because I don't believe these dogs had hearts; it was him, after all, who had fetched the boiling water that turned my body into the fuckin' mess I was in.

He told me they had agreed to give him £1,000 that was his cut for the use of the house. I was only to be held there for two hours at the most, he was told; when my time came, I would be taken to a second gaff. Although there I still was, five or six hours later, with no signs of moving. I pretended to sympathise with him and told him they were dogs for doing that and were bang out of order. He responded well, so I tried to coax the truth out of him. Where were they planning to take me? What were they up to? Who else was involved? But he just clammed up. All he would say was, 'I just do what they say... just do what they say.'

His arse had carried. He was terrified of them, and because of this, it was preventing my way out in a serious way, so I tried to get right into him.

'Look, kid, I'll take care of you,' I said.

He still didn't really know who I was. I was just a name and a body. Being a scumbag off the streets he didn't know the score on the old school and the way we worked. I tried to tell him I had a big crew behind me and he would have good protection from these so-called mates of his.

'Look,' I kept saying, 'let us out of here and I'll protect you; I've got plenty of back up. Nothing can happen to you. Listen to me! The others don't give two fucks about you. The other two might even put one in you just to get that other grand back!' For all I knew, that was what they were planning. The more I spoke, the more nervous he got, until he was sitting in that chair like a zombie. He was as thick as two short planks. He just didn't have it all upstairs. I had one last try at working on this fucked-up smack-head... one last try to have it away out of here. He had already told me his first name; Brian, so I began trying my hardest to manipulate him once again.

'Listen Bri, you *do* know that they are using you don't you? I mean you even went and picked the money up for them. That's really sticking your neck out.'

'I know,' he replied, 'I know, but what the fuck can I do? By the way, it was your kid [brother] who passed me the money. He had a go at me.'

'Why what happened? What did he say?' I asked impatiently.

'I never forget a face, and if anything happens to my brother I'll hunt you down, and make sure we cop for you. Remember that! And another thing; I want to hear from our Charlie at every hour, no matter what time it is; I wanna keep tracks on him.'

'That's what our crew are like Brian. All my brothers and mates are dead loyal to one another. Why don't you listen to me? Untie me, help me get away. I've told you before; you can come with me, I'll make sure you're looked after... come on kid. Help me!'

'I can't, I can't, they'll fuckin' kill me. I've told you what they're like.'

'Brian lad, look what they've done to me, I'm in a bad way. If I die you *do* know it'll be a murder wrap? And *you're* implicated with them if that happens.'

He paused for a minute, trying to think with his fucked up head. Then he turned to face me with a weird look and a trace of sarcasm in his voice he said,

'What they have done to you is fuck all compared to what Alan has done to the others.'

'What do you mean? What others? It couldn't have been as bad as this! Go on then, what could be worse than this?'

'Alright then, a few months ago they had a fella in here just like you, and Alan poured boiling water over the man's dick and balls,' he said with a bit of a smirk. 'They were all welded together. He even shoved red hot curling tongs up his arse. He was in a terrible state.'

So, I thought to myself, I'm not the first that has been brought to this scruffy hole of a place. This is the torture chamber that I'm sitting in here. I've got to get myself out. Somehow or other I've got to get myself out of here, and fast!

'What happened to him after that Brian?'

'His wife came with the money and he was taken to some ozzy [hospital] out the way. See what I mean, you had betta go along with them. I'm warning ya, you had betta get your kid to pull the money up.'

I couldn't control my hatred for this bastard and the rest of the scum.

'Alright, I can see now that you're not going to help me, are you? Well fuck you as well... you're only interested in the money!'

He clammed up straight away after me shouting at him. He then turned around and pulled out his jacking up gear from one of the drawers to start injecting himself again. Knowing I was fighting a losing battle, I gave up on him.

Shortly after, the others arrived back looking pleased with themselves. I noticed they had changed their clothes and looked a lot more relaxed. Lea, particularly, had a whole new demeanour. I was pretty sure the black fella had spoken to him and sorted him out. Lea was carrying a box of bottles; beers and spirits, and his clothes were clean and free from blood or any other incriminating forensics. He looked at me in my blood-soaked shirt that stuck to my back, the burnt flesh on my legs, my face all smashed in, still strapped to the chair without trousers. He walked over to me.

'Here, Charl...' he said.

Who the fuck did he think he was? I couldn't believe the Jekyll and Hyde nature of this animal. He was transformed. Mind you, I shouldn't have been surprised with everything that was going on. As I looked closer, his eyes were glazed. I was sure that the black fella had had a good chat to him about calming down and taking it easy.

'Hey, Charl, do you want a takeaway?'

I couldn't believe that he thought this was time for a party! I was sitting in the dirtiest room I'd ever been in in my life, with cat crap on the floor, litter, empty beer bottles, broken furniture, blood, and cat hair from Airey's beast. How the fuck do you sit and eat in a hole like this without washing yourself and the stinking room first?

As I look back, it's hard not to think about how this would never have happened in my day. These animals have no compassion, no understanding and no restraint. Worst of all, they've got no consistency in their slimy work. Working out on me one minute and then trying to treat me like one of their friends the next! That was no sophisticated mind-game; that was not being able to make up their *own* minds. If they had been half tidy criminals thirty years ago, there's no way they would have gone about this with mad destructive methods. It just wouldn't be done like this.

Whenever I got involved in a bit of graft, whether it was my own job or as part of another team, I always relied on professional planning and decision-making to get us the maximum reward with the minimum risk. And with a good crew on board, and a good plan to work to, it meant you could afford to be flexible if things went pear-shaped.

I remembered the way I used to do it. Back at the end of 1965, I was becoming well-known and respected for my approach to the work, we got to know a lot of people from different parts of the country. I would get a call from a mate down south or it could be up north with something tasty for us. Sometimes, local Firms can't do a job on their own doorstep, as they might be under police surveillance. If a job was pulled, they were the first suspects to be picked up by the police. The only way you do have a chance of doing anything in your own area is to leave the town as soon as the job is done, stay low for a few weeks, and then if you *do* get lifted for it, by then memories have faded a bit and witnesses are hard to find.

To have one of these heavy jobs away, they have to be planned meticulously. You have to have the right men; with plenty of bottle and not too erratic in their behaviour. By that I mean; if a job doesn't look right when you are about to strike and you get a sixth sense that something is wrong; then it is best to leave it and just walk away. By doing this, you can stay free to thieve another day. It is no good moaning later on if you get nicked saying, 'I should have done this, or that.' You cannot afford to come unstuck on one of these heavy jobs because if you are caught, you are going to go to jail for a very long time.... but that was back then!

Despite my private fears for my life, and the pain from my burns and beatings, I was still able to maintain the mental strength that has got me out of so many difficult situations in the past. The pack of dogs who'd been throwing my brother's money around in front of me had little or no regard for the lessons I'd learnt, and I cursed myself for having let myself fall into their pathetic hands so easily. They were unprepared, unsure about each stage of the game, and clearly didn't trust each other. Here I was, sitting in this disgusting hell hole, tied to a chair with my body on fire from the scalding water, and they were trying to convince me and Joe that they were genuine hard-cases. But if they were proper fuckin' psychos, why are they trying to play it the other way making out they were good fellas? Turning on the fuckin' charm. Why show weakness? They were playing at this and the sad thing was; this was no torture den they were using just for today, or any other day for that matter. They were used to eating here, to being here. One of them lived here for fuck's sake! I watched them poke about in this filthy little room and heard them rattle around upstairs for about half-an-hour until Airey returned with the scran (food). These two grabbed at it as soon as he was through the door and just sat there, eating, as if nothing was out of the ordinary. They were definitely used to living like this. This was their way of life. A world of dirty backstabbing work, of filth and abuse. They weren't building anything with the money they made, they weren't improving their lives, or anyone else's for that matter.

Airey settled himself into the chair opposite, sitting the way a teenage girl does, all curled up. He called that cat of his in a girl's voice and it came and settled itself on his lap. I looked over at the other two who had finished eating. The black fella was motionless but Lea stood up, wiping his greasy mouth and went and spat on the floor, the uncouth bastard started getting down on a bottle of shorts that was half-empty. As I watched him, he started to stare back at me, a contest that was broken by Airey walking between us, holding the cat. I listened to Airey's footsteps climb the stairs and then the floorboards above my head creaked. The walls in cheap houses like that are like cardboard and I could hear every movement he made. That house was so full of holes, I'm sure if I could have stretched my neck backwards I would have been able to see him above me.

A repetitive knocking noise could be heard coming from upstairs where Airey had gone to his bedroom with his cat. Lea, still drinking from the bottle, pulled a face and looked up to the ceiling, he then looked back at me.

'He's fuckin' at it again up there.' Then he looked up at the ceiling and shouted,

'Hey, dirty arse are you fuckin' that cat again?'

I couldn't believe what I was hearing here, if Lea was right and Airey was doing that to the cat; he has gone the lowest a human being can go. With his fucked up mind he has resorted to bestiality, the filthy scum is into animals! It made me want to vomit.

As for Lea; he's just as bad, in fact in my opinion far worse; what sort of a man, if you could call him that, can torture another by mutilating his private parts, and I now know I am not the first he has done it too. Is it because he gets off on doing it? Is that a cover up to hide his real sexual deviancy? Because let's face it any person that gets pleasure from doing that... it must be!

As the night wore on, the black fella who had been sitting talking to Lea left the house and Airey still hadn't come down from upstairs. I was once again left with Lea. He again started to tell me how remorseful he was; he was so fucked up from the drink that he could hardly speak but I wasn't sure if that was what provoked his sudden rush of guilt. Whenever I was left alone with him, I thought how I'd helped him in prison and how he had repaid me.

He was probably doing the same, thinking about what a cowardly fuckin' thing he had done by betraying me. I just sat there and watched that fuckin' pathetic, drunk piece of filth as he tried to seek forgiveness. No way would I ever trust this rat. But he came and sat close to me.

'Charlie,' he said, 'I'm going to tell it to you straight. I'm gonna help you get off later on tonight.'

I started to listen. 'Him upstairs, he can't know about it 'cause he'll open up on me to the black fella'

I wasn't convinced. I was pretty sure this was an attempt to encourage me to follow their plans. I knew he didn't want me causing any problems.

'I want you to slash me face, so it looks like you escaped after doing me in.'

Then he paused.

'I'm asking you one thing, Charlie, man to man... I know you're going to come back... but leave my tart and kids alone. If you want me, just get me.'

I couldn't believe it. This scumbag expected me to be as low as him. I'm no woman or child-beater. Of course, he was lying to me. Why would he stick his neck out to let me go, knowing full well I'd hunt him down? Remorse? Not from the likes of this dog. Even if he did feel bad, there was no way he'd endanger himself out of guilt. No, this just made me certain they had plans for me never to see my family again. Just like they had said before; they were going to put a bullet in my head. But Lea was drunk, which meant I still had a chance. Lea kept on talking, but I had stopped listening long ago. I was searching my brain for an idea, a way out of what was fast becoming the place in which I knew I would die.

Lea carried on drinking as he talked and was well off it, when all of a sudden the black fella steamed in. He looked at all the empty beer bottles and shouted,

'Has he been making the fuckin' phone calls? Don't tell me he hasn't!'

'What phone calls?' asked Lea.

Something had been forgotten. My brother had stipulated that I was to call him every hour so he knew I was still alive. The black fella had made this clear to the others, but obviously they had taken no notice. When they admitted they hadn't, the black fella went mad. Lea got up and started snarling at Airey who had reappeared, just as the black fella started screaming at Lea.

'You'll bring it on top you soft bastards!'

It was about three hours since I had last made a phone call to our Joe, so I knew this was dead serious. I was hoping no one would panic and try and put one in me there and then. When they eventually calmed down, they made me call my brother and reassure him I was OK, and then ask for another ten grand! I couldn't believe the cheek of these bastards. Again, the black fella held the phone to my mouth while Lea held a gun to the back of my head.

While all this had been going off, quite a lot had happened with our Joe. Using the tracking device, he had located the house where I was being held and had sat off the place. Ten or twelve of his, and my, associates had circled the place, tooled up but cautious. Joe had got dead wary, though. He knew they had loaded shooters around me constantly and he knew these dogs were in and out of the house all the time. He also didn't want to arouse any police suspicion and so pulled them out. He knew that if he and the lads tried to steam in, one of those dogs would have put a bullet in me. But now, with the phone call over three hours late, he was doing his nut. Certain friends and family who were there as advisers, agreed that it was most likely that I had been whacked, and convinced Joe of this fact. They all urged him to go to the bizzies as soon as possible.

Understandably, Joe wanted to hand over responsibility of the situation to someone else; now it looked like I was dead, so he and a few friends walked into Belle Vale Police Station where they reported my kidnap, torture and possible murder. Unknown to me, the whole situation was being explained to a team of bizzies just a few miles away and was becoming a major incident. The bizzies enforced a full media blackout; this is absolutely necessary with kidnap and torture, both international crimes.

While we had been sitting there, the police had made their way to Joe's cottage across fields from behind, so they couldn't be seen from the main road. They brought with them a considerable arsenal of weapons and technology, including phone taps, which were well in place by the time I had come to make the call. I sat there with a gun to my head, calling my brother, not knowing half of Merseyside Armed Response Team was listening in!

Our Joe was dead nervous, but he had good reason to be. We had kept him waiting for three hours.

'Charlie, you were supposed to ring hours ago, is everything all right?'

'Yeah.' I said. 'Listen, Joe, they want more money.'

Everything went quiet. Lea was so nervous he was starting to push my head forward with the barrel of the gun. Then my brother sighed and said, 'Yeah, Charlie, OK.'

And what he said next really did me in. 'I'm gonna sell me daughter's jewellery.'

They still thought Joe had plenty. They had beaten and tortured me and threatened me with death; and now they were going too far with my brother, and were taking money from his family.

Words cannot describe the fuckin' rage I experienced at that moment. I couldn't control myself. Fuck those dirty bastards, I'd had enough.

'Give them fuck all, Joe,' I shouted back. 'Don't give them anything else, the fuckin' animals!'

I didn't have time to tell him who it was. The phone was gone and suddenly Lea was on me. He was wild. He held the gun in my face and pressed his nose close to mine, snarling,

'I'll put one in you right now!'

But I had lost my head from the phone call and I started shouting back,

'Do it then, if you're gonna fuckin' do it!'

Again, it was the black fella who stepped in to calm everything down, but not until a further ten minutes of squabbling and accusations for forgetting the phone calls had passed.

Lea was shouting at Airey, but the black fella took control and brought him to his senses.

Looking back, I would always wonder why the bizzies didn't just storm the place; in their defence, they were well aware a gun was pointed at my head all the time. But, then again, bizzies are bizzies. If a villain shoots another villain, they couldn't care less. It's just another dead villain as far as they're concerned.

It was up to me to make another phone call with the same setup. I was still totally unaware that the police were listening in. I had calmed down now, too, and was wary of Lea, the crazy bastard, putting one in me. My brother told me there was a few more grand, and I told him the drop-off circumstances would be the same. This gang of rats got to work again, this time in dead silence. Three blank faces, eyes down, moved quickly about in that dark room. What were they up to? No one spoke.

This was the second time this particular operation had been executed in the last twelve hours. All three faces were emotionless, no one even blinked as they prepared. I watched each one of these dogs as they geared themselves up, ready to go and rob my brother. My head throbbing with pain, I could no longer feel anything below my waist. I thought I would need a couple of years of physiotherapy after it was all over, assuming I made it to hospital.

They were ready to leave, but something seemed to be holding them up. Every time two of them were out of the room together, I strained my ears to catch any part of the conversation. I knew they were talking about me, but I heard nothing. At one point, they all left the room at the same time. I don't know what they were doing but I watched the door without moving a single muscle. Lea finally walked in. He didn't even look at me. If he had done, I'm sure he would have seen that my whole body was stiff as a board, getting ready just in case. I don't know why, but it just felt like it had been going on for too long. I hadn't slept or eaten for many hours and had been strapped to the chair so long I couldn't have moved if they had released me. Ever since I'd seen Lea with that shooter, I knew it could have happened at any time. I couldn't shake the feeling that had been with me for many hours. The strain was getting unbearable. I had to give myself a proper talking to, just to take control and stop myself from losing it. I didn't want to let them know I was feeling the pressure, they'd then have the edge and I'd be as good as dead. But I controlled it and told myself that if I kept my head I'd be all right. I was just so tired and the pain from my legs came in waves through my whole body. I had to stop myself from dropping off. All of a sudden I heard a voice:

'Come on, Brian, let's get going.'

It was the black fella, calling Airey by his first name. They were ready to go.

CHAPTER 8

We were now into the second day of my ordeal. To be precise, it was twenty-seven hours since I'd been lured into this hell-hole. They'd already had one 'success' with the first drop, but they wanted more, so the second pick-up was now getting under way.

Airey was again the bag-man (the one to make the pick-up). He came downstairs looking like death warmed up. He was tall, dead thin and pale. With his sunken cheeks, he looked worse now than he had done since I arrived at his filthy house. The lack of sleep would certainly have been getting to him by then. Having the strength to withstand a situation like that as it ran across days is not easy. When something like that went down, especially as they were pumped up, they all thought they were Superman, but the human body can't sustain it for long; particularly when you're in a dangerous situation; where everyone is on the edge the whole time. Lea, too, looked rough; he had a crazed look in his eyes and was grinding his teeth. Only the black fella stayed cool and determined. The three of them paced around me. Now and then, one would look at me, but only for a second. I think they were just checking I was still tied up. I have to admit, I myself was close to hallucinating.

I was in constant pain. My neck hung down with exhaustion, making my back and shoulders ache. My arms and hands were twisted and bound and were numb at the shoulders and excruciatingly sensitive at the wrist. My feet were bound and were swollen. The angle they were tied at was putting huge pressure on my already inflamed thighs. A full day had passed since that sick bastard Lea had poured boiling water over my body. My head throbbed constantly from the beating I had taken and my ears rushed with blood. My eyes felt hot and the muscles in my face ached from constantly watching them. I was desperate to relax but my nerves and reflexes were constantly on edge. I watched them just in case this was the moment they decided to whack me.

It's not possible to describe properly what it felt like. My body was in total panic, which numbed the pain for the first hour. By the second hour, I started to feel tired, by the third I was starting to ache badly and, by the fourth, all I could think of was the pain as I wondered how much longer it would last. I watched everything they did, hoping they would remain as tense as I was. I knew the minute they reached total exhaustion; their bodies would just give in. I've seen it before. The brain just starts doing weird things to cope with the strain. When someone gets like this they are at their most dangerous... temporary insanity. People get too tired to give a fuck and, if this happened, they would just stop caring about the money and about themselves. They certainly wouldn't give a fuck about me. I knew that if it went on too long, Lea would just whack me first and think later.

Airey stood there in front of the other two, in silence. Finally, he said,

'All right, I'm ready. My cat's gonna be alright here, innit?' Airey glanced nervously up at Lea who just stared at him. 'Yeah, your cat's gonna be OK soft arse. Now fuck off and get the money!'

Nobody moved and Lea's words hung in the air. His contempt for Airey had always been obvious; but he was starting to make no real distinction between his hatred of Airey and his hatred of me. This was a good thing. It made it more likely that Airey might help me have it away and also pushed Lea closer to me. It was his total lack of respect for Airey that made him hate him so much and, although he hated me, I knew he respected me. This meant they were getting weaker and weaker as a team, as paranoia was setting in. I was sure the black fella had given Lea a good talking to about being careful what was said in front of me, because he had been dead quiet since they last went out. But now he was letting things slip. He was tired, we all were; no one was thinking straight.

Because of this, I watched every move. Airey put the cat down nervously and it wandered away. I knew why he was wary. I had reluctantly made the phone call to my brother, forced with a gun to my head. Now Joe said he had more cash and fuck knows when it would end. I knew it was pointless arguing with these dogs; their brains were fucked up, though I never saw the black fella shouting. He never looked like he was losing it, like Airey and Lea. When it was time, he gave Airey a nod and said to Lea,

'You know the score if anything goes wrong.'

He said they would be at the pick-up site in twenty minutes and would have the money within the hour. I was left in the company of the vile bastard again, whom I despised more than anything.

I was now well into my second day in the chair. My body ached and was deteriorating rapidly. But I kept quiet. Lea obviously had no interest in talking to me. As soon as the others had left the room, he stayed silent. All I heard were a few street noises coming from outside. It was a day like any other and I could see Lea staring at the closed curtains, desperate to leave. Like me, he had had enough. He was getting fed up and it didn't take long for him to get on to me. He knew I was seething with hatred for him, much more than for the others. He watched me, smiling, as he had throughout the torture and pain, and I stared back. My expression had been calm before as I stared him out, but it was different now. I sat watching that scumbag drinking cold water in front of me and, as he stared at me, my face told him exactly how I felt. I knew I was letting my guard down, showing weakness. For years, I had always disciplined myself never to let an enemy know what I was thinking. But now I just didn't give a fuck and I could see he was enjoying every second.

Then he tried to start a conversation again. 'Are you alright, Charl?'

He was calling me Charl again, just to wind me up.

'Look, mate, what can I do?' He paused. 'You know the score. Like I told you before, I had no choice but to bring you here. It's out of my hands!'

Each time, he paused to see how I would respond.

'The black fella is running the show, you can see that. It's not me; you've seen what he's like.'

I just sat there thinking; you two-faced bastard; grassing on his own mate to me, just to fuckin' feel better; justifying his filthy actions to me again. But he could see he was getting nowhere with me; trying the come-on talk so he could distanced himself again.

He was sitting in a chair on the other side of the room facing the wall. I knew he was brooding over my silence; he hated the way I defied him. He sulked like that for ten minutes and I was starting to think he might stay like that until the others got back, when suddenly he jumped up and pulled out a shooter. He had had it tucked into his trousers, a big gun; a 45 revolver. I have handled one myself in the past and, believe me; one shot from a gun like that would have literally blown my brains out. I knew that if he shot me with that, it was the end. He approached me slowly with a snarling grin on his face. Then, slowly, he placed the barrel of the gun against my forehead. Leaning forward, he said quietly, 'I know what you're fuckin' thinking, Charlie. I'm not soft. I know you're going to come after me.'

He wasn't wrong; I'm not in the forgiving business and this wasn't making me feel any different. I just had to get out of there alive, and then my time would come. I thought back to times when I could have walked away, turned the other cheek, when the risks were massive, but the need to dispense my own form of justice was just too powerful too resist.

If this animal Lea had any inkling of what was going on in my head, he'd have known not to fuck with me. The three of them must have been talking about what I might do if I was released or if I escaped. I could see he was worked up.

As slowly as it was placed there, the gun was removed from my forehead and he took a half-step away from me and hunched up a little. I braced myself for a sudden movement but, even with this warning, I was caught off-guard by what followed. Lea spun round and thrust the revolver into my eye, laughing as he did it. He then turned slowly away and, all of a sudden, spun back and once again forced the loaded shooter into my face. The crazy bastard was playing a sort of Russian-roulette with me. He was so tensed up, the gun could have exploded in my face at any moment and I couldn't help but flinch and try and twist away in desperation at his manic movements. I knew what that kind of gun did to a face and I was scared... he was going mad! Every time he lunged, he let out a strange shout. I was just thinking, This is it! This is what my death will be: shot by a lunatic after a day tied to a chair.

Lea's eyes were crazy. I couldn't turn away. He was thrusting forward so viciously my face was starting to bruise. He shouted, 'I can blow you to fuckin' bits right now!'

I looked into his face, 'Are you going to put one of them in me?' I asked. 'Is this it? Are you the one who's going to do it?'

He stopped and pulled the gun away. Then he started to laugh.

'You don't think I'm fuckin' stupid, do ya? Your daughter saw you getting in my fuckin' car, I'm not that fuckin' daft. No, it won't be me who's going to whack you.'

But then he started doing it again, though with less energy. I knew he wasn't lying, but fuckin' about like that wouldn't stop the gun going off accidentally.

Suddenly, his mobile rang and he took it across the room to answer it. Calm as anything he said, 'Hello?'

Then there was silence as he listened to what the other caller said to him. I thought it must have been the others with a problem. Maybe my brother had not shown up. Maybe he had brought less money, or a shooter. The police station wasn't far away; I wondered if this was the call to tell Lea to kill me and get the fuck out!

But Lea looked calm enough. He started pulling faces and I could see he was annoyed by what the other person was saying. I realised he was talking to a woman. He just kept saying,

'Yeah, yeah, no, no, OK, yeah...'

It amused me to watch this dog bowing down to some woman. When he was finished, he threw the phone on the chair and walked back over to me.

'That's the other fella's ma,' he said.

The other fella was a mate of theirs, doing life for murder. Apparently, a man was stabbed to death up in Preston by a gang from Liverpool and he was one of the gang who got life. He is supposedly innocent of the murder and is awaiting an appeal.

Then Lea went on, 'I'm fuckin' fed up with her, we're always giving her money to keep him going in jail and she spends it all on doing her fuckin' house up. She thinks he's going to win his appeal, but he'll never get out. He's fucked!'

He said this with his eyes open wide and a mad look on his face.

Just then his phone rang again. He answered it and his face lit up instantly.

'Everything go OK? Thank fuck for that.'

It was the others; they were on their way back.

When the black fella and Airey came in, I couldn't believe what I saw. Airey was carrying a shiny, black briefcase containing the money. The three of them crowded round excitedly as it was opened. Again, the sight of money turned them into kids; everything else was forgotten instantly. But the minute I looked at the briefcase, I knew something wasn't right, though they just carried on as if nothing was wrong. When you're on a blag, you always have a sixth sense for things like that, you can smell them. And that suitcase reeked. My brother wouldn't put a paltry £7,000 in a big suspicious briefcase. He wasn't dropping to businessmen, he was dropping to scallies. And he certainly wouldn't be wearing a suit, so I was certain there was no way he would be so stupid outside a police station. It smelled of police involvement. (I know now that that was what was happening, but at the time I couldn't figure out how the bizzies could be involved.) It was dead obvious to me; only they would pull a daft move like that. That case, in those hands, in that house, stood out like a sore thumb. I knew that if I had gone to make a pick-up on a job, I would be wary of a black briefcase like that. I'd leave it there or at least take the money and dump the case. But we can't all think fast, can we? Especially not this bonehead Firm, who had me captured.

Lea was all excited again. He asked the black fella a few questions about the drop; was it suspicious, had anything gone off? All the while staring at the case. He snatched the case and ran upstairs with the black fella to count the money. They told Airey to wait downstairs and watch me. He walked over to the chair opposite me and sat down. He just watched me for a few minutes before saying, 'By the way, your kid still wants to hear from you every hour.'

I just nodded. Then he started to curl up on the chair and try and sleep, before suddenly leaping up and leaving the room. He must have remembered he had left his cat here with Lea and wanted to see if it was still alive. I heard Airey in another room, then footsteps came downstairs and I heard them whispering for a good five minutes. More footsteps came downstairs and others returned upstairs. All the while there was nervous whispering. I wondered whether the stupid police had got the amount wrong. I was certain it was their handiwork that led to a shiny, expensive briefcase being given to these idiots, especially when the first drop had been a satchel. I couldn't think of any reason why Joe would call them.

In the end, I assumed it must have been his mistake, or he just had nothing else to put the money in. I wondered if the black fella had got suspicious about the case upstairs and that they were going to come and grill me about it. I wasn't arsed; they could ask me all they liked and I knew even in this state they would be easy to fool. I kept listening. All I heard were more footsteps and bickering. Then silence.

I tried to listen harder and harder to hear what they were talking about but I could hear nothing. Then I felt something in my stomach start to turn over. My head started to spin and it was getting harder to think straight - I couldn't shake the feeling that was creeping into every part of my body. It was blind panic setting in. I knew they were up to something, I could feel it. I twisted and jerked in the chair to see if I could wrench my arms free, to no effect. I felt like I was being stalked by some horrible beast.

The last time those dogs had made the pick-up, the euphoria had lasted a whole night. They had gone berserk in uncontrollable excitement, throwing money around and shouting. They weren't shouting any more, they weren't even moaning about splitting the cash up. This could only mean one thing. They were ready to sack it all in. This was it. They were getting ready to kill me.

CHAPTER 9

Airey said my brother wanted to hear from me every hour. The black fella must have known that, and so would Lea. Yet there was no sound. None of the pandemonium of the phone call before, nervous voices, sweaty hands, the shooter pressed to my head. Why would they not be nervous about keeping our Joe happy unless it didn't matter anymore? They were coming for me and I couldn't do anything to defend myself. It's one thing to take on three men in a fight and lose, at least you've had the chance to get a few digs in and stand up for yourself. But to be unable to move, to be forced to watch them taking their time, powerless to do anything is fuckin' terrifying. To go through anything like this, you would have to be a man of steel.

I felt physically sick as I waited and waited. I knew what they would be saying. They would be talking about how to do it. Lea would be nodding, the black fella giving orders and Airey staring at the floor. I had watched them for two days; I knew them well by now, and I knew I didn't have a chance. All the hopes I'd had of escaping were going out of the window. None of the things I had thought of were going to work now. They were a team again, a pack of hunters - none of them really thinking, all just going on instinct. An instinct for survival. I didn't think I was going to die... I knew it. I had been expecting it for two days; two days of strain that had left my mind exhausted. I knew then I was about to see the gun that was going to kill me.

The three of them came into the room. They walked slowly and silently. I could see from the looks on their faces that I was right. None of them looked at me, they had been planning my execution and the black fella was again in control. He walked over to me and said,

'Look Charlie, I didn't know you properly before but I've heard good reports about you and you're supposed to be a sound fella.'

The gravity of the situation was starting to hit them; they had realised who I actually was.

'Charlie,' he said. 'We respect you as a man, but you know who we are now and that's just too bad.'

'What do you mean, what's wrong, what's going down?' In my mind I knew this was it!

He just looked at me in stony silence then raising his hand, he put the gun to my head and was readying himself to blow me away. I have faced death on many occasions, but this was the most serious. I was convinced I was about to be wiped out. Yeah, it is true; your life flashes in front of you. Thoughts of my late mother and sister entered my head, even a last-minute clutch at religion. Until you are faced with this, you can't imagine the thoughts that go through your head, no matter how brave you are, or how hard you think you are. The gun pressed hard against my temple. I screwed my eyes up, waiting for the explosion that would mean a bullet was entering my brain. I don't know why I did that; I knew I would never hear the gunshot that killed me. It is a reflex for people to brace themselves, but by the time the noise reaches your ears, the bullet has already entered your body. My head throbbed with pain as I tensed every muscle in my body. I knew death was just a moment away and could feel the black fella's arm straighten as he braced himself against the gun.

With my eyes closed, all I had to tell me what was happening around me were my ears. It was deathly silent. I knew there was going to be one terrible bang, so loud it would bring the neighbours out and then there would be chaos. It felt like he was waiting an eternity, but for all I know he paused for only a second; it's hard to tell, my mind was racing.

The funny thing was, I had been expecting it for so long, it was almost like relief. I knew that in a few seconds my legs wouldn't be in agony and I wouldn't be tied to a chair any more. I felt none of the rage for these bastards around me that I thought I would.

There was no time to; all my time was gone. All I saw was a blur of faces; my brothers, my parents, old friends and then Bridgett. Then, just before he was about to pull the trigger, I shouted to him.

'Just shoot me through the heart!' He hesitated for a split-second.

'I don't want my daughter to see my face in pieces when she identifies me.'

Turning slowly round to face him and opening my eyes. I stared up at his face, the cold, heavy barrel of the gun resting against my head. But I stayed calm, unblinking. The gunman shifted his weight and nodded lowering the gun, but before he could shoot me there was a shout from the back of the room.

'No! Don't kill him here. For fuck's sake, wait, just hang on. His daughter seen me when I was at his house, she seen him gettin' in my car, this will all be down to me. She fuckin' seen me! I was the last one he was with; I'll get done for the fuckin' murder! We'll have to think of another way.'

Airey started to protest to the black fella.

'I don't want him killed here! That wasn't part of the deal. You all told me you were takin' him somewhere else and burnin' his body later.'

They all started screaming and blaming each other.

In an instant, the black fella turned back to me and stared me right in the face. I stared back. I didn't give a fuck now and my face was like stone. He went to do it. Don't ask me how I know; I just saw it in his eyes.

His face stiffened... he wanted to do it... he tried to do it, and I just thought, 'This is it!'

I stared at him and waited... but as quickly as I saw the impulse go through him, he stopped.

He dropped his gun and turned away.

My mind just went dead weird. I couldn't believe how close I'd come to dying in that chair. They had lost their bottle and my life was saved. I sat there in shock. The three of them started pacing around the room. Airey went to find the cat and sat down with it, shaking and saying nothing. Lea kept looking around nervously; only the black fella found his composure again. He looked at Lea and said, 'He needs to make another phone call, now!'

The hour was up. The black fella stood over me and started giving me instructions. I knew he had at last come to his senses, he had done his homework on me over the last couple of days, that's for sure. He was the cleverest one out of that pack of dogs, he knew I had strong backing and that if I had been whacked; in no time at all they would have been hunted down one by one and shot to death. He said to me, 'Tell your kid we're lettin' you go.'

He also told me to tell him that it didn't matter about the rest of the money. This was just as well, since I knew our kid had no more to give them. But I couldn't help thinking about the fact that at the beginning they had demanded £100,000 and weren't budging an inch. Now they were settling for a measly £17,000. I think they were gutted; they knew quite well they had fucked up. The black fella got the phone and Lea stood next to me with the shooter.

I called Joe. He was made up to hear I was being released, though I knew he wouldn't relax until I was home. I asked him if he was alone in the house and he said he was. I knew this wasn't true since, at the very least, he would have some solid mates with him. I asked him if any of the family were there. He said there weren't, so I told him I would be coming to his house because I was in a bad way and I didn't want any of the family seeing me.

From that moment on, the scum were like different people. All the fight had gone out of them and they were on a comedown. It was getting dark by this time; it was the middle of November. None of them said anything until Lea told Airey to go down the road and get me a taxi. I couldn't believe it! If that's not putting them on top; bringing a taxi to a house where they had been holding someone with my injuries and half-dead at the time, I don't know what is! I thought to myself, What sort of fools are these? It wasn't the first time I had thought that.

As Airey left to get the taxi, Lea started to cut the industrial tape away from my legs and wrists, where it had been for two days. I couldn't move. The length of time I had been there had fucked my circulation, my muscles and my bones. I just fell to the floor. I couldn't walk at all. Slowly, the feeling started to come back and, as I heard the taxi pull up outside, I found the strength. I just wanted to get out of that place. As I pulled myself out of the door, Lea put his face close up to me and said,

'We know you'll try and have us but I'm letting you now, we'll cop for your kid Joe; he's easy to get... or your daughter. There's twenty of us and we'll burn you out any time we want.'

I took no notice of him. I didn't have the strength to think about his fuckin' threats. It was his last desperate move.

I more or less crawled out of that filthy torture den, past the door I had not seen since I was tricked through it nearly two days ago. The taxi driver nearly did one when he saw the state of me. I told him I would be all right and directed him to my brother's house.

'Are you sure you're OK?'

'Yeah, I'm OK,' I replied. 'It's them fuckers who won't be.' I let my eyes close. It was over for now!

It wasn't until we were about a mile away from that stinking hole that I started to relax a bit and realised I was out of it. My body was exhausted and I shivered with the cold. All I could think of now was getting even with those fuckin' scumbags who had inflicted so much pain on me and my family.

When the taxi pulled up outside our Joe's cottage, the night was pitch black. Inside the house, all the lights were out. I climbed out of the cab and said I was going in to get some money to pay him, but he said it was OK and just got off. I think he was scared. I limped up the path towards the front door and, just as I was about to knock, it swung open.

There was our kid, Joe. He just looked at me in shock. He led me into the lounge where he switched on the lights. I got a surprise; all my family and mates where there, but I knew there was something not right. No one smiled; everyone was just staring at me. The women; our Joan, my sister-in-law and the rest broke down when they saw my face; it was so swollen and black and blue. It was a horrible feeling. I wished they hadn't been there. I didn't want them seeing me like this. I started to lose it. I started shouting to our kid,

'I need a shooter, fast! It was that Alan Lea and his crew. I know where they are. I want to cop for him, right now, before they fuck off!'

All the women were becoming hysterical. I heard a noise at the back of the room and saw a crowd of bizzies surround me. I couldn't believe it. Most of them were armed and no one in the room had told me what was going on. I couldn't work out what was happening; I was that tired. I couldn't think straight.

'You're going nowhere, Charlie,' one of them shouted.

I looked at our Joe and said, 'What the fuck are these doing here?'

'I thought you were dead, kid,' he said. 'I thought you were dead with not hearing from you for hours yesterday. I had no choice but to bring them in. I thought you were dead, we all did.'

But his voice was getting faint. I was feeling dizzy, I needed medical treatment. I just felt like I couldn't move a single muscle. I could hardly stand up.

From this point, my memories are a blur. I remember being dragged into the back room the police were occupying, and standing in the middle of the floor with seven or eight armed police around me. They were dressed like commandos and one of them was unarmed. He carried a camera and when two of them had taken my clothes off, he started taking photographs. They said they were checking to see if I had a gun on me. What a joke!

I was half-dead and they were checking me for weapons. But it had to be done. My clothes were rotten and stuck to my legs. Me, my clothes, my wounds, all had to be photographed as evidence.

Minutes later, I was rushed into an ambulance and sped to the nearest hospital.

I remember little of my treatment. My body was bandaged heavily for days and I was confined to a hospital bed until the Tuesday. I lay there under guard of the police for two days, slowly recovering from the massive trauma my body had been through. I told them there was no need for me to be watched, that I obviously wasn't going anywhere, but they still kept me guarded. They said they were taking no chances. I was grilled as to what had happened and how I had sustained my injuries (as if they didn't know) but I couldn't concentrate. The last thing I wanted was to relive that fuckin' nightmare; I just wanted family around me.

One of the bizzies who was interviewing me told me the armed response had raided the house where I had been held. Airey and some other men had been arrested. The bizzies interviewing me said Airey seemed more worried and concerned about his cat than anything else, was he altogether with us or what? Lea and the black fella had gone. They had done one. I just put it all out of my head and, after two days, was back home.

Under good medical care, my strength began to return. The police kept coming round, mostly to pump me about the investigation. It turned out that the forensics search had recovered a stash of drugs and a shooter, the industrial tape that was still covered in blood and hair from my arms and legs and there was even blood in the hall and on the floor.

Apparently, even the boxes that had contained takeaways they ate were still where they had been left. Stupidly, Airey hadn't got shut of any of the evidence. The other man was released after the police proved he had been nowhere near the house at the time of kidnap. Until then, I had wondered if it was the fourth character that had never shown his face.

Now I was receiving the proper medical care I needed. Within two weeks of treatment, I was starting to move and walk properly. In that time, my wounds were healing well and my strength returned, but the scars I had were there to stay, a reminder of the ordeal. As the days passed, my thoughts turned away from my recovery and to the two still out there, still roaming around, spending my brother's money. As I grew stronger, all I could think about was revenge. I wanted to hunt them down... and put them down if necessary.

Hatred, when it comes to control the mind, is more powerful than any other feeling a person can have. At night, after my ordeal at the hands of Lea, Airey and that black fella, all I saw were their faces. I had been released from that house but in my dreams I was still tied to that chair, and I suffered their torture all over again.

I received a lot of support during that time, from loyal friends who only a few months before had been helping me on my release from prison. Many of them were villains, proper villains with dignity. When we got around the table, we agreed to find out where the kidnappers were hiding. Every one of us agreed they needed copping for and sorting out, once and for all. Information was getting back to me about other tortured people who these sick bastards had been at it with. It soon became apparent that people had been suffering at the hands of these beasts all over Liverpool.

I just took everything in that I heard and made my plans. The allegations I heard were sickening, I couldn't believe what they had been getting up to; and I thought I had seen them at their worst. But everything I heard just made me more and more determined to get these dogs and kill them if I had to!

Here are photographs of the appalling injuries inflicted on me during my torture ordeal. Others have not been included due to being the private parts of my anatomy and are a lot more horrific, therefore they have been omitted to avoid the more sensitive members of my family being upset at the shocking sight of them.

This facial photograph shows a knife wound inflicted when I was threatened that both of my eyes would be cut out.

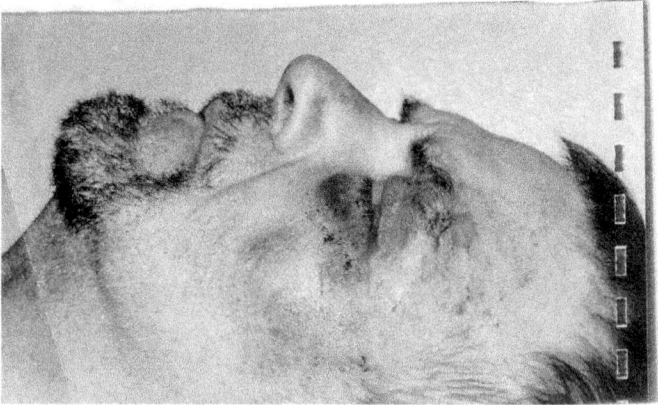

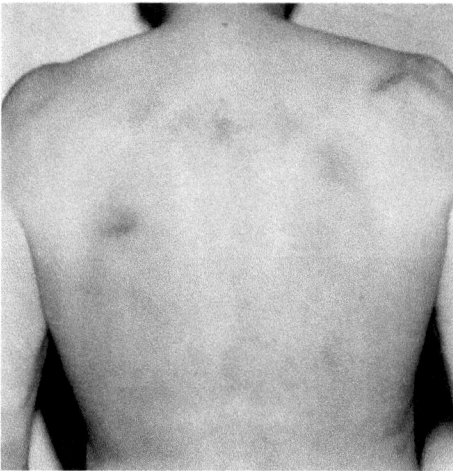

Vicious bite marks from where one of those sickbastards tried to rip lumps out of my back whilst laughing like a hyena.

The scalding burns on my lower anatomy where they poured boiling water over me.

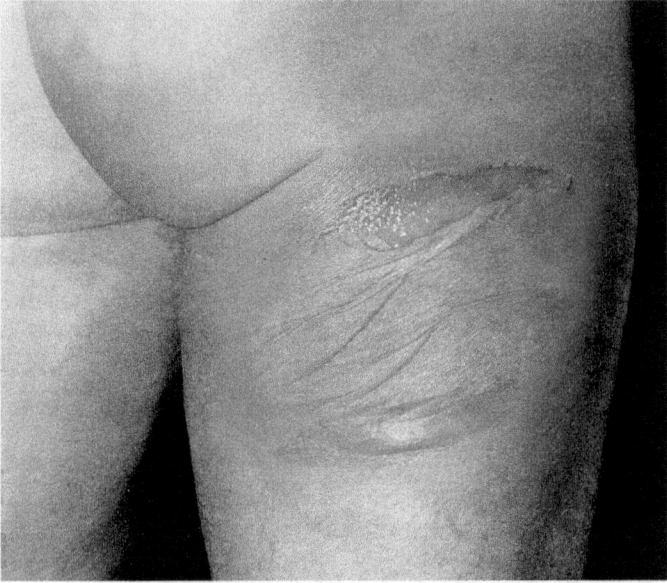

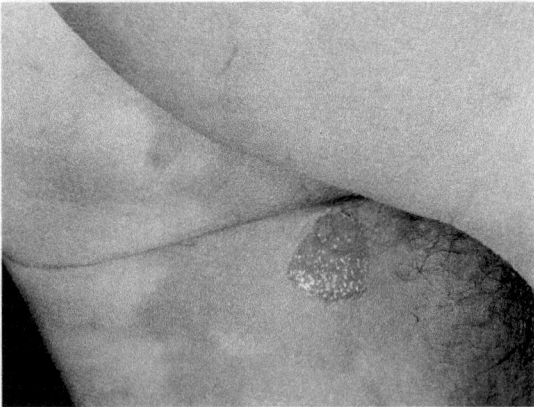

CHAPTER 10

I've come across some lowlife in my time: rapists, serial killers, paedophiles, you name it, I've seen them and done time with them and they've got the scars to prove it. But this was a first for me; being conned into spending 'quality' time in the company of the vilest scum I'd ever had the misfortune to clap eyes on. And to think I'd taken pity on one of them. That it was my generosity and consideration towards him inside that had led me to that shithole; and this was how the bastard repaid me. I cursed the day I responded to Alan Lea's shouts from the block, and vowed never to be taken in quite so easily again.

That's the difference between the old villains and some of the scum today. We were like anybody else; we had limits, there were things we weren't prepared to do. The need to hunt them down and get those bastards was boiling up inside me. That evening I met with a good crowd of mates and we all got our heads together in Huyton. From a house there, we started to put feelers out trying to locate Lea and the black fella.

We had a good mate who owned a scanner. He got a kick out of listening to all the bizzies going about their business. Day and night he would just sit in his house and listen to them and relay any messages back to one of the lads. Out of the blue one day, we got a message that he'd picked up Lea's voice. He was in the process of calling his wife in Cantril Farm, now Stockbridge Village, telling her of his movements. We still have the tape recordings we made of that call and I have listened to them many times. Lea said to his wife, 'Yeah, all right it was me. I know I was with him but it's not all down to me, it was the other black cunt, he was the one who wanted to do all this!'

He was making excuses for the bad moves he had committed,

shifting the blame on to someone else and trying to put one over on his wife just as he had done to me; telling me he didn't want to do it. To think I had trusted that snake enough to get into a car with him.

The crowd of us sat around that scanner, all our ears straining to hear what he said, in case he slipped up and mentioned where he was hiding. Conveniently for us, Lea was lax with his security and he told his wife and us that he was in an out-of-town bedand-breakfast. He didn't say where, though, so we continued listening to him blabbering on. He said when he got home he would buy her and the kids some new clobber. I went mad, knowing that it was our Joe's money he was spending on that hotel and on his family. We heard him saying he had to go because his food had arrived.

'Fuckin' hell!' he shouted down the phone at her. 'Mushrooms. I hate fuckin' mushrooms!'

Just as we thought he had finished talking; he told his other half the exact time and date he was coming home. We all turned to look at each other, not believing what we had heard. We knew now when to get him. We had a time and a date; I was going to get the dog!

That night I slept more easily, never thinking about who else had a scanner... the bizzies. They had been listening-in themselves and so were on top of Lea before we could get near him. By the time we arrived on the day, the bizzies had already copped for him. They'd been sitting off the house for days. I was gutted. There was Lea banged up in a safe cell and looking like he'd stay there. It was mainly because the bizzies got lucky, and through his own stupidity, that he came unstuck. All I had to do was wait. As soon as the charges were withdrawn and the two of them were released, we would cop for them and really make a mess of that sick bastard.

Every day I waited for news. I could do little else; my mind was dead focused. It was getting to me; knowing that Lea and Airey were inside. I faced a crossroads; I wanted to kill all four of them, but I didn't know whether I wanted it badly enough to risk getting captured by the police and ending up inside on a murder rap. That could have been the last I'd see of them. I decided to stay put and get more information on them.

We had a terrible stroke of bad luck. Our Joe, who has been a hunter all of his life, was charged with the possession of a hunting shotgun he kept in the house. It makes you wonder where the bizzies got their information from. It was no secret our Joe had a variety of hunting weapons, such as crossbows and traps, but he was charged nevertheless. His only hope was to state that his brother had been kidnapped, that during my kidnapping ordeal he felt threatened and therefore had it around to protect his little girl from the scum. His only mitigation was me and the kidnapping. This put a lot of pressure on me. Not once in my life had I ever made a statement or testified, and I was determined I never would. Decent villains don't get up to that game. Not in a million years was I going to break the rules. But I had no choice and, after speaking to our Joe, I knew I had to be careful. It could fuck up all the plans I had been laying for months. By giving evidence I would be expected to identify and name them. If they went down, I would never get the chance to take out my revenge and all that waiting would have been for nothing.

There was no way I would give evidence against them and label myself as a grass. I didn't care what they had done. This was going to be sorted outside of the courts, the way I wanted. So I agreed to go to court on one condition, and I made this stipulation clear because it meant a lot to me; it was the only thing I could do; I said I would give evidence about my kidnapping ordeal but I would deny recognising Airey and Lea. I would say I had never seen them before. I would let them walk free and then I could hunt them down myself. I could see no other way round it.

During all of this I kept putting myself on offer and fronting up the clubs in Liverpool. Everybody in Liverpool who had heard of them wanted them dead in a bad way. They had to be stopped, once and for all. It wasn't an easy time for my family and me. I was completely distracted with catching this scum and it took up all my time. I was just lucky to have so many loyal friends helping out and always ready to lend a hand. I had good men around me: Lee, Joey, Whitey, Roger, all good men with dignity. I was still getting around the city, always listening, waiting and watching. I have always been a patient man, it's essential for the line of work I used to be in, but this was getting hard. I couldn't afford to relax for a second, but waiting for the trial had gone on for nearly nine months and in that time I had to keep my head.

All the while I was getting word about Lea and Airey. They were in custody and two of our mates were on remand in the same jail. They were keeping an eye on them, watching every move they made and relaying it back to us. They sent word out how Lea was swaggering around and shouting his mouth off saying, 'Charlie screamed like a pig when we had him in the house.'

He was also saying there was no way I would ever go to court and give evidence against them, and he was right. He knew the rules, even if he didn't follow them himself. He was saying I was past it, too old and didn't have the bottle, and when I heard this I had to keep my cool. He was dead convinced of his invincibility, and he had no idea of the hatred I had inside of me. I had waited for the better part of a year to see him out on the streets and I was not about to fuck it up now. I had it all planned out.

I remember being told that they had got a working over from some friends of mine inside, who had had a good go at them. But I wasn't interested. Black eyes and a few little bruises were no good to me. I wanted them dead!

Two days before the trial, I received a visit from the bizzies. They wanted to check I wasn't going to back out at the trial. Let's get one thing straight... I have no love whatsoever for the police. I didn't want a conviction; that was the last thing I wanted. All the waiting, all the plans I had made would have been useless if they got sent down. I told them what I was doing wasn't for them, it was for my own reasons.

Later that day, I had another visitor, a man I had known for many years, and whom I have a lot of respect for. He came to see me at home, and as a significant lawyer in Liverpool, he came across good information occasionally. He came to tell me that Lea had made a statement against me. He had made explicit claims that I was one of the biggest drug-dealers in Liverpool and that he had worked for me as a driver on jobs. He claimed I employed him as a driver on runs to make heroin deals.

I just sat there in silence taking it in. That slimy snake was at it again and it made me sick. But it didn't change my mind about testifying. I had waited too long to throw away what I had in place. This animal had tortured men and terrorised women and children; he had once looked on as an accomplice held an electric iron to the face of a ten-year-old girl threatening to burn her as her mother screamed in terror. He had shouted at the mother, 'Don't you think he'll do it?'

This dog, who extorted and manipulated to make money, was now trying to get me sent down for drug dealing. So what do you do? How the fuck do you deal with scum like this?

He had grassed me and fabricated evidence, but still I was determined not to point the finger at him in court. I could do nothing if they were in prison. I came under pressure from a lot of good people, encouraging me to see them put away. They said they were the scum of the earth, worse than paedophiles, and that the principles and rules didn't apply. The rules for villains didn't count. But that didn't make me feel any better. There was no way I would come down to this level by grassing and testifying.

The night before Airey and Lea's trial, a number of good friends came to my house to show support. They were all going to be there the next day, including Jimmy Muat's young son and a number of people who had been tortured by this scum. I still couldn't help thinking about all the other people who had been hurt by them. I know what I would have done if it had been one of my family - I would have had no second thoughts about hunting them down and killing them where I found them. But some people just do nothing. It was because nothing had been done about these scumbags that they kept getting away with it.

A man I know, who is a well-known Liverpool businessman, had a little girl who was brutally raped and molested for months until eventually the beast was exposed. She was barely a teenager. This man, who had plenty of money around him and knew most of the villains in Liverpool, discovered that the paedophile who had been abusing his daughter was a mate of one of his friends. And so what did he do? Nothing!

I spoke to him about it and said to him, 'Why don't you do something? You've got plenty of money. If you can't do it yourself get somebody to do it for you.'

He said he wanted to leave it up to the courts and the bizzies. That sick animal that was responsible got a lousy five years. That businessman was a friend of mine, but is not any more. I lost a lot of respect for him. He knew what that animal had been doing to his little girl over a period of time. The beast had even videoed his sick practices.

After this visit, friends of mine kept coming up to me, persuading me that Airey and Lea shouldn't be on the streets. I could understand why they were saying it, but there was no way I was going to lower myself. I still had self-respect and the way I do things doesn't change. It's the way villains have handled their business for years. Fuck them if they thought I'd give them a walkover. I was keeping to my rules, the rules we had all followed, that we all believed in. I would never, ever, grass and never give evidence. Never in a million years.

The next morning, I was on my way to court. I thought about Joe's trial in a few weeks. I couldn't wait for this to be over. I knew what the morning would be like; a dragged-out formality. The endless time-wasting and swearing-in can be worse than the questioning and I wasn't looking forward to it, but it was a means to an end. The TV and papers were there, always looking for something tasty to report.

Inside the building, I met a large crowd of supporters. They had been dead loyal and I will never forget that. I looked over at the defendants' families. Lea's mother and sister were sitting near the door to the court, along with another couple of family members. With them was a man whom I had never seen before and one of my friends told me it was someone Lea had been friendly with inside, who had come to give a bit of support. The whole group looked over at us, and particularly the fella who was with them, who thought he could intimidate us by glaring at us and snarling. I couldn't control myself. I walked right over to them and stared them out. They just turned away,

I looked over and saw Lea's sister rolling a cigarette in the corner. I couldn't believe the state of her, rolling a cigarette in court. Where was the self-respect? I couldn't be bothered even looking at them anymore, so I turned to my friends and family and prepared myself for the trial. I knew this wasn't going to be easy.

When we were called, it took a while to get everyone in. It was packed tight. As soon as I was through the door, I looked up at the dock to see them. I couldn't believe what I saw. Lea was sitting in court wearing sunglasses and had a dark suit on. He must have been trying to look like a gangster because no one trying to convince a jury of their innocence would dress like that. His head was shaved to nothing and he grinned as soon as he saw me. Airey sat next to him, looking like a typical druggy and staring at the floor. His head was also shaved. I couldn't believe it. I thought to myself: If they act like this, they'll end up getting sent down no matter what I do. Lea just watched me and I stared back. I thought, You have no fuckin' idea what's going to happen to you when you get out of here.

The trial began quicker than I expected, the lawyers seeing off the formalities swiftly. When I was called to the stand I didn't feel put out or anything. I have heard that some people are terrified of going into a witness box. Not me; I've just been there lots of times over the years, I walked into the witness box and was sworn in, then their defence immediately got to work. He started firing questions at me, trying to undermine me, and at first, I just let him get on with it, I didn't have to look at the prosecution or the faces of the police who had come to see me two days before. I held in my hands the entire case and I fully intended to fuck it up for them. I stayed calm and just answered the questions. I knew Lea's brief was just doing his job; a lawyer can be defending you in one court one month and prosecuting you in another the next. That's the nature of the legal system. But the questions he started asking me were dead iffy. I knew Lea had instructed him in what to say, portraying me as a drug-dealer.

I looked over at Lea and he continued to smile. He thought I'd never give evidence and he was right. I continued to answer the questions carefully. Lea had told the lawyer to accuse me of selling smack all over Liverpool. He named different parts of the city I was supposedly visiting to do deals, Lea saying he knew because he drove me there. The dirty little rat was stabbing me in the back in the courtroom, doing what a proper villain never does and what I was determined not to do. 'I have never dealt in drugs; I have done many things, but never that.'

Their argument was that I got my injuries in a drug deal that went wrong. I still intended to say nothing to incriminate them but the brief kept on. If Lea had used his head, he would have known that there was no need for this. He knew the ways of the old villains, enough to understand that I would never testify. That's why he thought he was dead safe. He was using the opportunity to try and ruin my name in front of my family, my friends, the court and the press.

I chose my words carefully in response to the questions. I denied all those accusations, and got myself ready to say it wasn't them who kidnapped me. But the lawyer kept going on and took us right up to lunch time. We adjourned for lunch and, after been hassled by some press, I made my way outside. As I was getting off, Jimmy Muat approached me.

'Charlie,' he said, 'what's wrong with you? Put the finger on these fuckin' dogs.'

I think he just wanted to see them go down. I told him I wanted to get them myself and I had waited too long for this.

'They're scum, Charlie,' he said. 'They're lying about you; they're trying to ruin your name.'

I told him that I still couldn't do what everyone wanted. Others came over and again tried to persuade me to send them down. They all knew my intentions; they knew what I had been saying for months. They said I was mad, but I was determined. It was only me in that box and I knew I had to go with my instincts.

And that was how I returned to the courtroom. Everyone filed back into court and I went back to the box and got ready to let them walk. I knew the scene that would follow; the press, their families, the police all going crazy at the evidence I was about to give.

As the questions started again, Lea stood there grinning over at me. He had no respect for me or anyone in that court. He thought I wouldn't turn up, but here I was all right, facing them. My mind was still on my brother's court case over the gun business; he could go down for five years because of those pricks. The lawyer started his questions again with me, then, he got heavy with his cross-examination. I looked at Lea. He was gloating but I knew deep down he would be scared. I knew that no amount of bottle will stop you feeling the pressure stood there; I had been on that very spot a year before and I knew what it felt like, looking at the people who hold your life in their hands. But I knew all he had to do was stay cool and keep his head. So I stood there and got ready to let this dog go.

But then he did the unthinkable. Just as his brief was about to ask another question, he started shouting from the dock.

'Take no notice of him!'

In front of the whole court, the judge, his lawyer, all the officials, the bizzies and the jury, he started a torrent of abuse.

'He's a killer! He's a gangster; he shot George Bromley three times in the head. He put three in his head! He killed him! Don't listen to a word he tells you!'

I stood there, not believing what I'd just heard. Well, if that's not cold-blooded grassing, what is?

So what we have here is a one-way traffic system. In other words; it's quite alright for them to roll over on me, but I'm supposed to do nothing and keep my mouth shut. After all, it's that scum who broke the rules, not me. As I sat watching their skilful defence lawyers, who had been trying their hardest to have these two animals acquitted, it made my blood boil. Thoughts went racing through my mind; if only their barristers really knew who they had been defending; two of the vilest beasts on the planet, who terrorised ordinary men, women and children in gangs. These were not your old-school villains who had a bit of decency and respect about them. No... these were the vilest lowlife scum of today's society.

As my mates were all sitting behind me, while I was still in the box, some of them were hissing to me,

'Charlie, what's the matter with you? Get them done. They're worse than sex cases, the dirty bastards!'

I listened to my friends and considered all this, especially knowing that these evil dogs wanted it all their own way by blowing me up in court saying I was a heroin dealer. I mean, it was bad enough them saying I was a contract killer; that I could live with, but heroin peddler... No, definitely not. People in Liverpool who know me, know I've never dealt in heroin - I am totally against that.

Nearly every person who has something to do with a Crown Court, whether it be a defence barrister, or a Crown Prosecutor, a witness on either side or even the judge himself, are all actors to a certain degree. They all act out their parts they have to play. Believe me; I should know. I have been there many times throughout my criminal past. Basically, it's about which side can convince the jury the best, through their acting, of course. Well, now it was my time and so I acted.

I had been getting quite a lot of stick that day by Lea and Airey's lawyers, mainly because of my past. I was being accused of fabricating evidence and words to the effect of 'you're a liar, you're this and that.' But let's not forget, I was not the one who was on trial, and if only their defence lawyers knew, I had no intention whatsoever of getting their scumbag clients done, then maybe those same two lawyers would not have come down on me so heavily with their cross-examination. Then again, they have a job to do; they have to play their part as well. It did cross my mind, though.

People who have been in this situation, especially women and children who have been mugged or even raped, get severely crossexamined and then a scumbag defence lawyer accuses them of lying or making it all up. Something should be changed in the law to protect the victims of these crimes... not the perpetrators.

After both their lawyers had finished with me, I just sort of paused for a moment and considered what Lea had shouted out, openly grassing me in court in cold blood. I thought of the accusations and the statement he made against me. I also thought of the sick acts he and his gang had planned for my daughter, which he had described to me in detail. Throughout my life as a villain, there were certain lines that had to be drawn, especially with those who had respect and dignity for one another.

These days, it's a completely different kettle of fish. There are no rules, no loyalties and no dignity, as far as I can tell its dog eat dog now. You're far more likely to see who can grass first or who can make a deal first.

So I started by saying:

'Look, members of the jury. They call this the witness box I'm standing in. I call it the truth box. I think you people know who's telling the truth here. You've heard my side of the story, now let's hear their side. That is of course, if they have the bottle to get up and give their evidence. Oh, and by the way,' I said, looking straight at the defendants, 'it's definitely those two sitting in the dock. I'm sure it was them.'

When I said that, the court went deadly quiet. I looked across at the two dogs, and by the looks on their faces you would have thought they had just been sentenced to death.

They thought I would never do that; they relied on my

honour... and believe me, I never would have... only they grassed on me and wanted it all their way... so I played them at their own filthy game. They gambled on my honour and like I said they were the ones who broke the rules, not me! The court adjourned for an hour at the lawyers' request to discuss with their clients what had happened. When we finally came back into court, I was informed that Airey had tried to do a deal. He was now willing to change his plea and evidence, but it was too late. The judge wasn't having any of it. They had both fucked themselves, especially when they were giving their evidence.

The next day, they were both found guilty and sentenced. Before sentence was passed, Airey was swaying in the dock.

He was given ten years and Lea got twelve years. The rest of the pack are still on the run. How long will they be running for? Who knows! Maybe someday, and I hope that day is not too far away, somebody will find the rat hole where they are living and hopefully kill them!

As for Lea, he shouldn't be alive. I hate him more than any living man. It's beyond me how he ever found a girlfriend and had children with her. To achieve something like that, surely a man has to have some kind of human feelings and a heart. I just don't believe that thing had any of those qualities. Instead, what we had there was a callous, remorseless bastard lacking in empathy and the ability to form warm emotional relationships with others, a person who functioned without conscience. How is he going to end up? Who knows?

Some months later, my brother Joe had to go on trial himself for being in possession of the gun found at his house. He pleaded guilty and was sent to prison for 18 months. Yet another headache these bastard hyenas had caused my family, because after all, my brother's only intention; like any true parent, was to protect his little daughter and family from the likes of the lowlife scum.

If you weigh it up properly, we are not allowed to take the law into our own hands, but instead, those marauding animals would be able to come in and kill the family. You're supposed to do nothing but phone the bizzies. But do they ever get there on time? Like fuck they do. I will always support my brother for the actions he took to protect his family. I would do the same thing myself; shoot dead any scum who laid their dirty fingers on any of my kids.

Soon after my brother's trial, the Criminal Injuries Board offered me a large amount of money. Obviously, I refused it, because it felt like blood money to me and I wouldn't accept a penny. I kept getting pressurised to accept it by the Social Services so I decided to donate it all to the North-East Liverpool Victim Support Scheme; but I stipulated that it must only go to women and young kids who had gone through rape ordeals and other brutal crimes, when they have been at the mercy of people like those sick, lowlife scum.

Victim Support
Mr C Seiga
6 Valescourt Road
West Derby
Liverpool
L12 9EX

Victim Support

25th October 00

Dear Mr Seiga,

The management committee, staff and volunteers of the North East Liverpool
Victim Support Scheme would like to thank you for the donation of your entire
Criminal Injuries Compensation Award.

Our Co-ordinator informs me that you wish the donation to go to help female
survivors of Rape and Sexual Assault. To this end the majority of your award
has been sent to the Merseyside Development Office for Victim Support as a
contribution to their Female Rape Training Programme. This will enable our
organisation to train volunteers across Merseyside to support survivors
through their trauma.

Once again thank you for your generosity.

Yours Sincerely,

Frank McFarlane
Chairman

North East Liverpool Victim Support Scheme
Holly Lodge Girls School. 1st Floor, Uplands Building,
Queens Drive, Liverpool L13 OHE
Telephone: 0151 228 6769 Fax: 0151 259 8080
Co-ordinator: Janet Whitby
Registered Charity No 1013443

*Charlie regarded the payment he received as blood money and so he donated it to one of
the charities he supports; women and children who are victims of crimes such as this.*

I would like to make one other point clear. I never did what I did to help the bizzies. The thing is, as far as I'm concerned, they're still bizzies to me. I know we have to have some form of law and order but, like I said; I have no love for them whatsoever.

CHAPTER 11

I don't want to confuse fear with caution here, but every city in this country has these lowlife predators now, and their breed is growing. These types are the worst criminals of today's society; they are so sick and evil in their heads that they would think nothing of selling a child to a paedophile if it meant making them a living. They would brutally beat up and torture a pensioner whether it was an old man or an old woman. It doesn't matter to them even if it means killing, as long as they can get some money.

Let's say you are just a decent, average person, or a married man with kids, and these lowlife scum are on your case and they have sussed you out thinking you have money. What would you do? How could you protect yourself and family, especially if you weren't into violence and were the timid type?

I suppose that like any other upright citizen you would call the police; but the police are never around these days. You would most probably have been beaten up or even killed, before the bizzies got to you. Everybody knows that the bizzies know what they are up against with this sort of crime going on. But all they can do themselves is complain that the Government is not giving them enough funds, they are short of men, and so on. They turn a blind eye and take the easy option, leaving ordinary citizens to face the scum.

These days, crime is way out of control, especially as there are more violent rapes, muggings and killings than there ever were in my time. What we have now are two very different breeds of criminal. As daft as it may seem, we still have the decent villain, men who still possess a bit of dignity and honour, although these days there aren't many of them around. These are villains who would not share loyalty with the scum, but would go to the aid of someone being violently mugged or a woman about to be raped. They have much more in common with the villains I remember.

Occasionally, I still have a drink and a chat to some of these young decent types, earning their living in their own sort of way, 'a bit of this and a bit of that', and good luck to them as long as they are not hurting or stealing from the ordinary person in the street.

Then we have the other kind, the predators that wait and watch every move, trying to sniff out some of these half-tidy villains who may have had a touch and made a few quid. They will then try and have them off. These lowlife dogs don't give a fuck who you are; even if you have a strong reputation as a hardcase they don't care, reputations mean nothing to them, especially when there is a drug-crazed pack of them on to you and armed with shooters. What chance have you got? You might consider taking revenge on them but these animals don't give a fuck about comebacks.

Hunting this scum down is hard work. My friends and I have, on many occasions, tried to have them placed, but finding the bastards isn't easy. They are always on the move, ducking and diving. Unfortunately, there is always someone who will protect them, someone who will hide them until it's all blown over. For all the good decent people, it only takes one to hide a scumbag and keep their kind going.

Because of this, what we have now is a war, a conflict going on with two different breeds of criminal. One breed still retains the old ways and gets out and earns his money and the other, the scavenger, wants to take it from him even if it means killing for it. Two or three years ago, there was the word 'taxing' being used by the criminal fraternity. Taxing means villains who take off weaker villains.

Oh, by the way, these villains can't earn money themselves, they haven't got the brains or the arse to go out and plan a big robbery or any other job for that matter. They are just robbers' ponces. But like everything else, the taxing game is getting played out for them, so they move up the ladder where the prizes are much higher. Kidnappings, tortures and, more so murders are what have become big prize money to them these days. It is becoming big business. This sort of graft is mostly carried out by drug-fuelled gangs and is becoming more and more common now.

The bizzies don't know how to handle it, while all killings are on the increase. The number of murders that have been carried out in Liverpool over the last three to four years is unbelievable. This sort of back-stabbing crime is always on the increase and it's not carried out by young tearaways trying to impress older villains, no way. It's done for one thing and one thing only... money. They say nearly every man has his price when it comes to money. If somebody rips a person off, he usually gets killed, while the killer or killers get paid.

Don't get me wrong, money has always been important to me, just as it is important to every person. Every father has to be able to feed his family, every mother needs to clothe her children. But money is not the only thing I care about. Even when you're robbing, you're going home to a family and you're doing it with decent friends who you trust. You take pride in doing it properly and not hurting ordinary people in the process. But for these scum, money is the be-all and end-all. It is the bottom line and so they sell each other to the dogs day after day.

As I have mentioned before, my ordeal was nothing compared to what some sick bastards have done to some half-tidy villains over the past couple of years or so. Two young men in particular, whose parents I knew well from the older days (we all grew up in Huyton) they both had wives and kids and were betrayed and tricked just like it was by scum just like those who attacked me. They were kidnapped and what the poor bastards went through at the hands of this murderous scum was horrific. It was beyond human imagination. They were both severely tortured, slowly and agonisingly. I was told one of these poor kids had petrol poured into his mouth and ignited while he was still alive. The flames burnt his lips, his tongue and inside his mouth, his nostrils, his throat and much of his face.

You can only imagine the pain he must have suffered and this was carried out to extract money from that young man who, by the way, didn't have a penny. It's quite obvious; don't you think that if these young men had any money they would have parted with it rather than go through all that horrific mutilation? They were both found shot dead afterwards and both of their bodies were set alight and half-burned. These two decent kids were not hard-cases, they were not into violence, and they were not bigtime in any sort of way; just two ordinary kids who made a few quid here and there doing no harm to anybody. Both of these men's families still can't come to terms with what happened. Their wives are completely traumatised. All this happened just a couple of years ago.

Another young Liverpool villain, whom I knew quite well and who also possessed dignity and abided by our same high principles, was severely tortured and mutilated and died an agonising death. His limbs were literally hacked from his body, his torso was later found floating in the sea off the Spanish coast, of all places. How he ended up there is a mystery.

There is no need for these senseless killings. Those that I have mentioned are only the tip of the iceberg. There are plenty more murders which have been going on in Liverpool. There seems to be no respect.

There are certain kinds of murders I do fully agree with, though. For example, if a paedophile kills a little child and the father goes and shoots the bastard, well, good luck to him. And if some sick bastard killed your mother, brother or any member of your family, the bastard deserves to die. I would get him myself. But I have no time for these other sick, senseless killings. When will it end? Who knows?

This is the way of life for the modern, young tearaway of today; it's the day of the gun culture - kill or be killed!

Thankfully, I survived my ordeal and it is long behind me now. I was lucky - I was strong enough to get through it and get back to normal pretty quickly. The nightmares are long gone and now I am left with dreams of revenge. I can never forget what happened, and even though I have found normality, there is a side of me that keeps taking me back to that house, that wants to see an end to it - to see them pay for what they did. Revenge is sweet. As long as I get revenge, no matter how long it takes, to me it's the most satisfying sensation there is.

CHAPTER 12

Let me take you back to 1997-98. I had been caged up for twelve months in a Category A prison. It was while I was there that I decided to write down my memories. I did it mainly for therapeutic reasons, but also to relieve the endless, boring routine in that confinement.

As I've mentioned earlier, the stress of living under a Cat A regime can send some cons under, for good. In the first few months on remand, I witnessed a few who had cracked up. One reason which makes it hard is when you have become friendly with somebody and they come back from court after being sentenced to life or to 20-odd years or so. Some of them are in deep shock and have to go on strong medication.

With all this going on around me, I knew that I had to stay strong and think positive, not just for myself but for my family and my daughter. After all, they themselves were under a lot of stress. I found help to get through the ordeal from an unexpected place, after I had been almost five months on Cat A remand. It was coming up to Easter 1998, and my trial wouldn't begin for at least another seven to eight months.

The prison had a small classroom on this Cat A wing, and prisoners were invited to join if they wanted to brush up on their Maths or English, or any other subject they cared to study. I decided to join, solely to keep my mind occupied.

The prison had appointed a couple of outside teachers for this particular class; one was a lady called Val, and the other was a man called Alan. They were both fairly pleasant and I would describe my relationship with them as friendly. Alan said to me one day:

'Charlie, you seem to hold a good conversation and you've been around quite a bit. Why don't you write a story or maybe your memoirs? After all, you have the time on your hands and it will take your mind off your case or trial.'

I thought it was an excellent idea at first, then paranoia set in. I lost my head a little bit, I thought this could be a trick, anything I write about such as a bit of villainy could be used in court against me later on. Being on a Cat A wing, you cannot afford to trust anybody. Alan then reassured me, and so did Val, that everything would be OK and nobody would know what I was writing about. They said as far as they were concerned, I would just be brushing up on my English.

Well, that's how it all began. Val and Alan would give me little exercise books and I would just write and write, sometimes in my cell late at night. Each time I filled up one of these little exercise books, it would be smuggled out of the prison, don't ask me how. Alan and Val were two nice, down-to-earth people to me. They gave me a lot of inspiration and encouragement to continue recording my experiences. It helped me considerably at the time and, although I didn't know it then, it was setting me up for my life outside as well.

I had written well over half my autobiography when I was finally found not guilty of the contract killing of which I was so wrongfully accused. By the way, God bless that lovely, compassionate Liverpool jury... I will never forget them.

A few months after my release, I had the pleasure of meeting a lovely young lady; I will call her my 'beautiful friend'. She would frequently call to my home and we would have the odd glass of wine together, play some music, have a laugh and just chill out. Even though she was years younger than me, it didn't matter - we just really enjoyed each other's company. But what I found quite amazing about her was the inspiration she gave me regarding my first book.

It all came about on one of those lovely evenings we were spending together. She already knew about my background and what I had been going through. I explained to her how I had done a bit of writing while I was banged up. Let me make it quite clear,

I had absolutely no intention of becoming a writer; I was just dead happy to be free again when I was released and so who wants to write? Not me. I just threw it aside and forgot all about it until I met this young lady who asked to see it. She took it home with her and the very next evening she was back, only this time she was more excited. She said to me, 'Charlie, this is a brilliant story! It's exciting and well written, why don't you get it published?'

I told her I just didn't have the know-how to go about it all. That's where she came up with her expertise. She has quite a lot to do with certain TV writers and, being a bit of a celebrity herself, has quite a bit of influence.

First, she introduced me to some TV writer. I remember that day vividly; the first meeting I had with that bloke was a near disaster. Sometimes I have no patience at all with sarcastic and ill-mannered people and this man was just like that. He was having a party at his home when I first met him. I remember him sitting at a big dining table with all his entourage around him. After being introduced, I passed him my book. It was only in transcript form at that time. On doing this, the cheeky bastard turned on me and said, 'Look, I'm a very busy man. It will take me weeks to get around to reading this,' and he tossed the manuscript on the table in front of him.

There was no need for this behaviour, or the way he spoke to me in front of his guests. I sort of lost it and was about to pick my book up. I was just about to say to him, 'Fuck you, you sarcastic prick!' and then fuck off out of there, but my lady friend squeezed my arm and gave me a sort of look, as if to say, 'Calm down, take it easy.' She took my hand and we both went to the other side of the room and stood there. 'Just chill out,' she told me, 'everything will be all right, he always gets obstinate at times, it's just his way.'

'You should have at least prepared me for this.' I retorted.

I was fuming, but watching him like a hawk at the same time. After a few minutes or so, I noticed he was looking down at my book, and he began to browse through the first page, but still half talking to his friends at the same time. He must have been on to the third page when suddenly he got up and, picking up my book, walked over to another room which looked like a study. He went in and closed the door behind him. I looked at my friend; she just shrugged and said everything would be fine. After about ten minutes or so, he reappeared from his study, looked over to me and said, 'Charlie, can I have a word?'

His whole attitude had changed. I walked across to him.

'Look, Charlie', he said, 'I can see this is a very powerful story. This book should get published.'

And that is how I became a writer!

Basically, it's like everything else when you're trying to establish something for yourself. It's not what you know, it's who you know and, of course, how you go about it. So now here I am with a top TV writer who is literally bending over backwards to help me out. But let's not kid ourselves; these people don't do favours for you; they always want something in return.

Naturally, he's yet another significant figure in my life who wants to remain anonymous, simply because he doesn't want to be associated with a gangster and the stigma that goes with it. Funny though, don't you think, these sorts like to socialise with you when it suits them or when they want a bit of their dirty work doing? But to give him his due, he did send my book off to a variety of publishers. I remember him saying to me, 'All this can take weeks, possibly months. Publishers are very slow giving you an answer so don't get despondent. Be patient, it does take time.'

A few days later, he was on the phone to me, all excited. 'Charlie, I can't believe how this has happened so quickly! We've got feedback from some publishers already.'

He then rattled some of their names off, but one in particular stood out from the rest, the name was John Blake. I told him to sack the others and give it to Blake. I wanted them to have top priority because they knew all about the criminal fraternity and a large number of their books have been about crime.

One week later, I was on my way to London to sign a contract for my book to be published by John Blake. When I finally arrived at my destination, I remember being ushered into some fairly plush, office-type lounge. People were sitting around in there, all Blake's staff, and John Blake himself was there as well, obviously all waiting to see this Liverpool gangster that they had heard so much about. When I walked into that room, I could see from their faces they were a bit disappointed by my appearance, or rather amazed by me. It was a funny sort of atmosphere.

I glanced around at the walls which were all adorned with large photos of all the old London gangsters. Each one of the faces was made to look frightening and intimidating. I resembled none of them in any way. I am a fairly average man; 5ft 9in, 13st and I certainly don't look very hard, but that's only my opinion. Like I've mentioned, the atmosphere was uncomfortable. They were all used to having gangsters come into their offices but I had never been in a publisher's office with a book I had written before and, for a few moments, everybody eyed everybody else up.

They were all waiting to see me after all, and so must have been talking about me before I arrived, speculating about what I might be like. No one said anything so I decided to deal with the dismayed looks on these people's faces, and break the ice by saying:

'I bet you all thought I was going to look about 6ft 6in with a big gold watch hanging down by my knuckles and looking like those big yard dogs whose photos are on the walls. Well, I'm so sorry to have disappointed you all.'

With that they all burst out laughing. That started the ball rolling and we all got down to business. One of the staff told me they had to prepare the contracts and asked me if I would like to think about it first. They asked whether I would mind calling back in a couple of hours to consider it carefully, or maybe I would like to make some phone calls to ask advice. I said, 'Yeah, OK, I will have a walk around outside and have a think about it.'

I was a bit broke at the time and would have signed there and then if they'd only known. So I went to some cafes nearby and in those two hours I must have drunk a dozen cups of coffee.

Two hours later I had signed my first book for publication, and was on the train back to Liverpool travelling first class, with a cheque worth a few grand. It was an incredibly feeling, and one that I still get today when people ask me about the book. I am proud of it, but I don't go around looking for attention. Occasionally, though, someone will say hello after recognising my face from the cover and it reminds you that you've done something special, something that some people say has really affected them.

Since that day, when I went to Blake's in London and left a published writer, my life has changed dramatically. After publication, the book went on to become a best-seller, and is still selling strongly today. The only real change the publishers made to my story was to change the title from *The True Story of a Liverpool Villain* to *'Killer'*. I suppose they knew what they were doing; they are the experts after all. Besides, I had signed the contract, which I was going to honour.

Right after all of this happened, my entire outlook on life changed. I had the press and TV on my case all wanting stories about me and my criminal past and literary future, 'Why had I started writing?' and 'Had I left crime for good?' That sort of stuff. Some of the interviews I gave were OK but some got a bit personal. I remember being asked about my criminal past and then 'Was I a killer?' and 'Did I kill anybody?' I told them only what I wanted them to know. I have often seen all these so-called gangsters being interviewed on TV and some blatantly admitting to murder. If that's not putting yourself on top, I don't know what is!

In my opinion, there can be only two reasons why a man goes on TV and admits to that; either he wants recognition or he's lost it; in other words, he's plain fuckin' stupid. I would never reveal my innermost thoughts and secrets to anyone. They'll go to the grave with me.

These days, my life is so different to the way it used to be. People whom I didn't know before, most of them celebrities, are always inviting me to all kinds of events and parties. I am forever being asked to go on TV talk shows. I have done quite a few of them, but there were some even I refused to do, simply because, apart from being a pain in the arse, some can turn out to be like a stupid pantomime. Some people in the media are interested in you because of the history or because they are looking at loads of old villains and what made them what they are. They want to show the real person behind the name. Others just want to use shock tactics to sell papers or whatever, and they want to stigmatise you and your name further. People like that you can smell a mile off.

I remember the first one of these talk shows I did. It was being held at the Liverpool School of Performing Arts. Little did I realise what it would entail. I had to sit with a panel of TV writers and authors; Jimmy McGovern was sitting next to me. Jimmy is well known, both in Liverpool and throughout the UK, as a film and television writer. I remember him shaking my hand and introducing himself to me. As we all sat down on the panel, the TV crew had their cameras focusing in on us all. One of the attendants opened the doors for the audience to come in and the room was soon filled. There wasn't enough seating capacity so the rest of the crowd had to stand at the back. I was thinking to myself, 'What do I do? How would I start speaking?' I mean, nothing at all had been rehearsed; everything was right off the cuff.

When everyone had settled down, the speaker from the panel started to address the crowd. First, he introduced each one of us and explained that we were all good crime writers and all had books published that had become bestsellers. He then went on to explain that each author would take their turn to describe how they became a writer and that, after that, questions could be asked to specific people on the panel. I was just sitting there trying to take everything in, not realising what was about to happen. Just as I was thinking, God, I hope I'm last, the speaker suddenly turned round to me and said, 'We will now give you... Charlie Seiga.'

I was completely taken by surprise. I was struck dumb and a bit apprehensive at the same time. I am not frightened of many things, but this experience was terrifying me. I thought, What the fuck do I say or do now? I thought the other writers would have been chosen to speak before me; that would have given me some sort of clue as to what it was all about, as well as given me a bit of confidence at the same time. So here I was, facing this big crowd and you could have cut the air with a knife. It was dead quiet, the whole room waiting for me to speak. I looked at the sea of blank faces, and the cameras recording every little thing I did and said. I was sweating terribly under the lights; a Gestapo interrogation would have been easier.

So I began by saying, 'Hello, everyone, I am Charlie Seiga. I have to tell you, I have never done anything like this before so could you all just bear with me and I will try to explain in the best way I can.'

After all, most of those people were your intellectual type, being from the University and the Performing Arts school. I started telling them how nervous I was facing a crowd this big. I also told them I would sooner be facing a judge and jury, and the outcome of my trial and fate. Having said that, they all started laughing and I don't know why, clapping at the same time.

'I started writing while I was in jail,' I told them, and then explained in full, how I started writing and got the book published. After telling them all this, I then added:

'I don't think I have done anything really clever by writing a book. After all I only wrote about myself and my past experiences when I was involved with crime. It was no big deal or anything as far as my writing goes, in fact, it was all dead easy for me. I would find it a lot harder to be one of these good authors here. They have to think hard and make a story up. Now that's what I call real talent, but me, I just told my story the way it was and the way I actually did it with no holds barred.'

When I had finished my speech, it was then the other crime writers' turn. They all explained how they became crime writers, but it was starting to get hot and stuffy in that place. The TV cameras were practically on top of us and it really felt like I was the object of a big interrogation from the bizzies.

Then we eventually got to question time, when the audience could ask the panel anything they liked. When they started, it was incredible; everyone was asking *me* questions most of the time. The other writers were just sitting there, mostly being ignored. I actually felt a bit embarrassed for them; every time I finished answering a question, somebody would put their hand up wanting to ask me another. It seemed they were more interested in a villain's life and what made a person like me tick.

Most of the questions I rattled off were dead easy to answer and, by this time, I was brimming with confidence, but then some of the questions began to get personal and tricky to respond to. I remember two in particular from that evening. I had noticed a party of women sitting in the front row of the audience. They had caught my eye when they came in, and continued to throughout the show. One of these ladies looked a cut above the rest, she had been watching me the whole time, quite unpleasantly and with a calm, fixed gaze. She stared directly at me and said in a well-spoken but quite cold voice:

'I would like to ask Charlie Seiga a question please.' She continued quite briskly. 'I have read your book and you talk quite openly about your life of crime and particularly about the armed robberies you have committed. I have a post office where the staff and myself were held up by an armed gang, and I can tell you, Charlie Seiga, that it was a terrifying experience.'

She paused here and seemed to compose herself. I was worried she was about to cry.

'I was just wondering how you feel when you commit this sort of crime and have these ordinary, innocent people scared to death.'

After she had finished, she sat back with a sort of stern look on her face waiting for an answer. It had all gone quiet; you could have heard a pin drop in that room. I thought to myself, How the fuck do you answer that? I was put right on the spot with no way out of it. There wasn't a person in that room who wasn't hanging on my response; everyone wanted to know how I would answer this one. I knew I had to choose my words carefully.

'Look, love,' I began, 'for your information I have never committed an armed robbery on a Post Office and I never would, simply because they don't have enough money on the premises. You and I both know that the average flow of cash through a post office is about ten or fifteen grand, at the most. It just would not be worth the risk for me and my friends to stick our necks out for a small amount like that. The cut wouldn't be big enough to go around four or five men. Now if it was a Post Office van, yes, maybe. A bank or a big sorting office possibly because they carry large amounts of readies, but not your average little POs.'

I paused in the silence of the room. Nobody moved an inch. I then said to her, 'I am what you'd call a reformed villain now. I've finished with crime. But if I did have a change of heart and went into your post office to do a 'blag' and I saw you in there with your lovely blonde hair and beautiful blue eyes, I would just forget about the money and grab hold of you and take you far away with me forever.'

She started laughing with the rest of the audience and they all started clapping. Thankfully, she did have a sense of humour after all.

My next and final question came from a right knobhead, a Scouser trying to talk posh. You know the type I'm on about, sitting there in the front row in his Woolies shirt and tie and trying to pronounce his H's as he spoke. He began by saying, 'I have worked all my life and I have worked very hard. I wouldn't want the likes of your type stealing from me or my family whom I have provided for all my life. I hate people like you who have never done an honest day's work in your life.'

I suppose he was right in a way; it is quite true I have lived off crime, but there's crime and then there's crime. I have never robbed the ordinary man or woman, or anybody poor or who's having a hard time. I knew what this character's game was all about; he wanted a pat on the back making out to the audience that he was a good, upright citizen. Maybe he was, but his whole attitude was out of order.

'Look, pal, are you still employed?' I asked him. He nodded. 'Where do you work?'

He said he was employed in some big firm of accountants, so I said to him:

'You know, mate, I chose to become what I was, a robber as you say, but that was down to nobody else but me, and do you know the reason why I chose that way of life? Because I didn't want to become what you are, a zombie; clocking on and clocking off all of my life. What are your rewards at the end of it all? A gold watch, and that's if you're lucky. Or maybe a pension and a handshake. I have nothing against you for what they call 'choosing the right path' and working honestly for a living. I have got nothing against anybody who chooses to go out and work for somebody else. But, you see, I couldn't live that endless, boring routine existence. I have always wanted the good things in life and I have gone out and got them. Some great philosopher once said that the greatest secret of enjoyment in life is to live dangerously, and that's just what I did and I don't regret it one bit. Anyway, mate, get real. Why would I want to rob from you? You've got nothing to rob.'

When I finished, he just shook his head.

The show finally came to an end and my friends and I went out for a drink in the local bar. It was good to get out from under the lights, and I was pleased it was over. It just so happened that there were quite a few TV celebs in there who had been watching the show. Some big guy who was in their company came over and introduced himself. His name was Colin McKeown, a famous TV and film producer. He came right to the point and said he had read my book and thought it was an exciting and well-written story. He wanted to set up a meeting with regard to doing a film deal on my life story, and he invited me back to a party; and what a party it was. There were dozens of celebrities there, and loads of women, it was like a scene from a film itself, all of us drinking champagne until the small hours.

The following week, we had that meeting where he told me that *Killer* would make a great six-part TV drama. He told me that he thought it was a powerful narrative and that I shouldn't rule out the idea of it becoming a major feature film. He told me he saw large things potentially and said he would draw up a contract if I was interested. What could I say? Of course I was interested, who wouldn't be? But then I never bank on a promise. It's not that I'm a pessimist or anything it's just being cautions from past experiences. Business is like that whether you're selling a story or a car. There are two words, so they saying goes, 'fame' and 'fortune'. Well, I'm not interested in the silly fame side of it, only the fortune and, if I can make a few quid from it, well, that will do me.

Colin *did* keep his promise and we now have a contract ready to sign, but making a film isn't like writing a book. All you need to write a book is a pen, some paper and an imagination. Needless to say, you need a fair bit more than that to make a film so things aren't off the ground yet. Agreeing a script is the first stage and that can be difficult; a lot of people have to be pleased. But once the legalities are sorted, hopefully we can make a killing.

CHAPTER 13

I think most people have heard of the name Kray, or the Kray twins, as they were more commonly known, two villains from the East End of London who were in their prime and heyday in the 1960s. Kate married the late Ronnie Kray, who died in prison after being caged up for a staggering thirty plus years. What a liberty that was. Here is a man who never harmed the ordinary man or woman in the street and never harmed a child. His crime? He was supposed to have shot and killed two men who were out and out bullies, yet there have been many more horrendous murders committed against women and kids by sick, perverted animals and what do they get? Paroled and set free after serving a few years, frequently re-offending in the process. Why weren't the Krays paroled? Because the parole board and the government kept insisting they were still a danger to society. How could they be a threat to the public? They were two old men who were both dying and had served over thirty years. This was a liberty if ever there was one.

As for Kate, she never faltered. She stayed strong and no matter what certain people have said or what ridiculous stories have been made up about her marrying a notorious gangster, that was her and Ronnie's business and nobody else's. One thing's for sure; she was there for him right up to the very end, giving respect and her undying loyalty. I remember the first meeting I had with Kate Kray. I was down on a business trip in London and she asked if she could see me. She walked into some big office I was sitting in and she came right over to me with a big smile on her face.

'Hi, Charlie,' she said, 'I've read your book and I've been dying to see you.'

She kept talking and talking, wanting to know all the ins and outs, and before long we were chatting away and laughing like old friends. She was always laughing. No wonder Ronnie married her; she must have given him a lot of inspiration and happiness in his last years. Eventually, she moved on to a more serious note, wanting to know how I tick and what it was like in the older days compared to now, meaning crime, of course. I explained to her what it was really like for us in Liverpool, especially in the 1960s when we were all in our prime and bang at it.

Incidentally, there is a rumour that I have heard more than once that the Krays came to Liverpool by train and were met at Lime Street by a Liverpool villain, Tacker Comerford, who told them not to get off if they knew what was good for them. The rumour, as I have heard it told, had them stay on the train and return to London terrified. I want to make clear here and now that the story is a lie.

Firstly, I know Tacker Comerford and he is not into violence and never has been. In fact, he couldn't fight to save his own life and I know for a fact he never said those words to the Krays. Here is the real story and the full truth about that vicious rumour: The Krays did come to Liverpool, but they stayed for about two days, and it was strictly business. Around that time, a lot of Liverpool clubs had been granted gambling casino licenses and the Krays came to sniff around. I am not entirely sure why; maybe they were thinking about expanding a little by opening a place in Liverpool and getting someone to front it for them, who knows?

Anyway, I remember all my mates were following them around the city at the time; we were all still young men in our early twenties. They and most of their crew were dressed dead smart, but then so were we. Every young villain in the 1960s always wore nice, expensive suits and shirts; it was a sharp, clean way to dress and we all kept up that image. The Krays were well into their boxing at that time and there was a fight taking place on the second night they were there. Of course, every villain in Liverpool was there; most of my mates were sitting around the Krays in the stadium, and the atmosphere was terrific. There were that many villains in the stadium that night that if the devil had thrown a net around them all he would have had a good catch!

My mate Tony was sitting next to Ronnie, and after a few bouts there was an interval. The usherettes came around the punters carrying trays of drinks and food. Tony helped himself to a pork pie and was about to take a bite when Ronnie turned to him and said laughing his head off, 'Fuckin' hell, Tony, don't eat that pie, it might be a bit of Ginger Marks!'

Ginger Marks was a London villain who was killed in a gangland execution. His body was supposed to have been put through a meat mincer and fed to pigs on some farm.

Later, when the boxing had finished, our crowd and the Krays' crew decided to go to some nightclubs. At that time, the Shakespeare was the big attraction in Liverpool. It had good cabaret acts and served good food, and was thought to be plush at the time. When we arrived, everything was laid on for us. Now don't forget, all the Liverpool villains are on their best behaviour trying in a nice sort of way to impress the Krays and show a bit of respect for them and their Firm. We all settled down and the cabaret started, everything was going fine, until the unthinkable happened.

Apparently, two women started arguing and that turned into a full-on fight. A couple of fellas went to calm them down but, in the confusion, somebody else got involved and the next minute all hell broke loose, a right big kick off. Everybody piled in. It turned out to be a right bloodbath; chairs, bottles, anything was used as a missile or weapon. The Krays just sat there in a stony silence and there, right in front of them, was a man trying to tear another man's ear off with his teeth! There was blood everywhere and the Krays did the sensible thing, they quietly got up and did one (departed).

Later on, they apparently said, 'Fuck these Scousers, they're not interested in money, they just want to fight and kill one another. Fuck trying to set anything up in this city.'

They got the train back to London the next day, but at no

point were they chased out of Liverpool; they went of their own accord.

It was stories like this one that Kate Kray and I chatted about in London, taking the piss out of one another at the same time but all in good spirit. You know what it's like when Scousers and Cockneys get together, always feeling each other out. We are definitely two different breeds though, that's for sure.

'Charlie, will you come on my TV show?' Kate eventually asked me. 'It's called *Hard Bastards.*'

I looked at her. 'Oh, so this is what it's all about,' I replied, 'trying to get me on telly, on that silly soft bastards show.'

She started laughing. What would I do? With her strong persuasion, I finally agreed, on the condition that I would not be portrayed as a hard man and a fool. She said I would not. A few weeks later, she came to Liverpool with the TV crew to start shooting. Little did I know I was going to regret this for the rest of my life. Before signing anything, I should have made sure I had control over the edit. No matter what you say on camera, it can always be altered in the edit and I should have tried to make sure I could stop bits going in that I didn't want, but it was out of my hands. I don't blame Kate; she is as much at the mercy of the editors as me.

So there I was boosting Liverpool and saying how warm and friendly the people are, but that obviously like any city we have some lowlife scum. The majority of Liverpool people are brilliant in every way. I went on to mention the beautiful buildings and architecture and even bragged about Liverpool FC, but all of this was cut out. Another disappointing part was when my friends and I took the cameras to see the nightclub scene to show everyone how fantastic the nightlife is in Liverpool. This was cut, as was the book signing in Waterstones. It was dead sly and devious the way they worked that one on me. Instead, they had me going around in the daytime on camera, not looking too good. I was wearing some old casual clothes at the time and I remember them saying to me, 'Don't worry, we'll do the good parts later on tonight.' But they cut all the good parts out and instead had me looking like a *Big Issue* seller.

I swore after making that *Hard Bastards* I would never go on the TV again unless I had the editorial rights. I have got nothing against Kate for all that went on; it was completely out of her hands. I will say that she was great through it all though, and we did have some laughs when being filmed together. We became great friends, Kate and I, and she invited me to stay at her home for a few days with a girlfriend. Just recently she sent me Ronnie Kray's favourite tie. She said he always wore it and, out of respect, she wanted me to have it.

On the back of *Hard Bastards,* I started getting more offers to talk on other TV shows but I refused them point-blank. One in particular that I refused was the *Trisha* show. Their agents were offering me a tempting few quid and the opportunity to make some good publicity for myself, and I was about to accept it as well, but, lucky for me, and through good info, I found out what it all really entailed.

First, they were going to ask me questions and try and get me to admit to cold-blooded murder; that contract killing in Liverpool, and then ask me if I'd ever done any other murders. It was true that I was charged with a contract killing in Liverpool and it is also true that I have been investigated regarding other murders, but that doesn't make me a killer and I certainly wasn't going to admit that on national TV. To say something like that would be madness. I maintain and always will that I have never killed anyone.

The other reason why I rejected this totally ridiculous talk show was because they wanted me to sit between two other supposed 'villains', one of whom I discovered was a fuckin' paedophile who would be talking openly about his crime and how he was innocent of it all; of course, like they all do! The other person who would be sitting next to me was supposed to be a London gangster. His job was debt collecting; I believe he used to go around wearing gold-plated knuckle dusters knocking fuck out of people who couldn't pay up... isn't he dead hard? No. I sacked that Trisha and her clowns off. It would have turned out to be a lousy circus show; especially if I had kicked off and battered that paedophile sitting next to me.

So this is how my life is to date; film deals are on the table, celebrities number amongst my circle of friends and some of my days are filled with engagements to speak on literary panels at academic institutions. I even have authors who write to me, and whom I sometimes socialise with. Some of these writers though can be a bit of a pain in the arse at times; always wanting to know the ins and outs of everything regarding my background. 'Did you really kill somebody, Charlie?' 'What was it like?' 'Did you really rob a bank?' 'How did it feel?' and so on. I think some of these writers are just curious about the real way of life, the real crime; after all, they have to make their stories up.

One writer I did have the pleasure to meet was Martina Cole. She was different from the others; she never tried to blag me and ask me all kinds of ridiculous questions. She didn't have to; she lives in the real world. Here is a woman who comes from an ordinary, working-class background and had no help from anybody; not that she needed any, she's much too strong for that. She started writing and in no time at all became a best-selling author. I think she has had about eight or nine books published; what an achievement that is. Martina Cole is one of the most charismatic, talented women I have ever met and I am honoured to have her as a friend.

Although this new way of life for me does have its good points, there are times when I think about the past. It will always be there, never to go away, not just for me but for other people, too... the bizzies for example. Even though I am well out of the crime business and have been for years, I'm still not off their hook, and the bizzies will never let that happen. Only recently, two dogs; out and out bullies, had been at it terrorising some decent people and what happens? One of these dogs gets shot at. The bullet missed him, more's the pity, but apparently these bullies go running to the bizzies and make a statement naming me and a mate of mine saying we were going to shoot them. What a load of bollocks. If I was going to shoot somebody, and I'm saying *if,* I certainly wouldn't be broadcasting it around or giving them a warning first.

The bizzies came round to my house and gave me a letter warning me that if any more shootings occurred in the area they would be coming back. What the fuck was I supposed to do about that? I wasn't even responsible.

I've had plenty of experience of this kind of treatment at the hands of the bizzies. I've known some decent ones, but the years have shown me just how far they're prepared to go to get what they want, and the authorities, the courts and juries are usually willing to give them the benefit of the doubt.

In 1963, I went for trial at Liverpool Crown Court. I had been involved in a bust-up in a nightclub and had gone to sort out one of the culprits later at his house. I had a shotgun with me and was a little surprised, to say the least, when his front door was opened by a copper. I pleaded not guilty to the possession and intent to use a firearm, but I had no chance. The police identified me, although a gun was never produced. Some policeman stated that, while I was in custody, I had boasted to him that I had meant to shoot one of them. This was total lies, of course. There were no taped interviews then. It was all based on verbal, which was one of the most dreaded phrases any villain could wish for in those days. A policeman could state in court that you had told him you had committed the offence and this might have been completely untrue and, no matter how much you protested, they would always take the bizzie's word saying, 'Our police don't tell lies.' I was eventually sentenced to three years on the basis of that copper's version of 'the truth'.

There was a general mood at the time among the population, of the police needing to be protected from the likes of us, *'After all the police were as honest as they come and would never swear a man's life away would they?'* and whatever they did must have been approved by the 'higher ups'. That was great for the bizzies, as they had a field day nailing virtually whoever they wanted just by picking a fight with them, and then making them look like crazed police-killers when it came to court.

Most magistrates are just puppets in a court. Some of them don't even understand the law properly. The magistrates' work varies when they are not sitting on the bench. In fact, I've known a certain magistrate to be working behind a supermarket counter and another in a pet shop. One was even a retired school teacher. The majority of these people don't know the first thing about the law and yet they have the power to deprive you of your liberty, even if you are innocent. But it's the police who pull the strings. They are all just kangaroo courts and they will never change. Even to this day, it is still going on, and I believe it's going on more than ever before.

Law and order is essential to our society. Our mothers, sisters and children wouldn't be able to walk the streets freely if we didn't have law and order. Not that our streets are safe now! But the law must be enforced in a proper manner if we, the public, are to uphold and respect the very community it is controlled by.

As you can imagine, I don't have a great deal of faith in the honesty and integrity of the police force in general and now I was being hounded again. Soon after I got that letter telling me the bizzies would be after me if there was another shooting in the area, there they were, humiliating me again, knocking on my door. This time it was about a murder that had occurred in a pub named the Yew Tree that's not too far from where I live. Someone had gone inside ballied up and he had shot a man dead. Obviously, the bizzies have to make enquiries, I have nothing against that, but why come to me all the time? Their excuse was, 'We are working on a theory, Charlie. We believe the gunman was after you. He might have thought the man he killed was you. After all, Charlie, you have some enemies and there's a contract out on you.'

It is true, I have one or two enemies, lowlife scum; the type whom I have been fighting all my life, but as far as the contract goes, since I was told about it several years have passed by and

I'm still around. I haven't gone anywhere; I'm still in the same house in the same area. I'm not on the run, but some of the scum enemies of mine are.

Like I've said, the past won't let go of me and it doesn't help that the press and TV spotlight has wildly exaggerated all the rumours and stories over the past couple of years. Now I have some people calling round to my house asking me for a bit of advice, or even sending me mail from different parts of the country wanting counsel. I will help, as long as they are decent people, because it is not money these people are asking for, it is just that they need help badly. Some have been brutally beaten up by animals, and others are too terrified to go out of their homes because yobs are giving them a dog's life.

I got one letter recently from down south; an old man was being held prisoner in his own flat. He wrote telling me he'd been mugged and beaten up on several occasions. It had got so bad that he didn't know whether he was coming or going. It's so sad, but unfortunately, I am not a miracle worker. I would love to go down there with a few of the boys and knock fuck out of these lowlife scumbags but I have to be careful these days. I know the bizzies are waiting for just one slip to bring an end to my freedom once again.

Dear Charlie,

I had to write to you and thank you for looking after us on our trip to Liverpool. And a big thank you for taking part in my forthcoming TV series – 'Hard Bastards'. When the head of Channel 5 watched your show - he decided then and there that your show would be shown first. He thought it riveting viewing and admired your honesty. The show has only scratched the surface of your life and, after reading your brilliant book, I am convinced that your story would make a compelling film.

Obviously, before I met you I had heard your name many times and heard lots of stories of Charlie Seiga, some good, some not so good. But everyone agreed on the same thing: that you are a fair man. I gave you my word that I would not portray you as a hard man and I won't. I will only speak as I find and will end this letter this letter as I finish your chapter in my book.

Charlie is a man who has done a lot of things in his life, always for a good reason – in his eyes. The way I see it he is no angel. Then again, he is no devil either. We'll leave it at that. One thing for sure is that he is a gentleman. Recently, I had to go to Liverpool and Charlie and his friends met me. There was a limo waiting at the station and I have to say that I was treated like a princess.

Maybe it's called Liverpool hospitality. I'm not sure. Devil? Killer? But gentleman, definitely.

Thanks again Charlie. God Bless.

Lady Kray

CHAPTER 14

Well, I am now at another crossroads. I thought it was about time I moved on, so I decided to put my house on the market, what with all the hassle from the bizzies and everything else that was going on; there were also a number of other reasons why I wanted to move out. I had been living there for four years after the murder with which I'd been charged and that stigma would never leave the house or me while I was still there. Even four years on, people still slowed right down in their cars when they passed my house and, out of morbid curiosity, would try to get a good look inside, straining to see the room where a man was shot three times, or catch a glimpse of the man who'd been acquitted of it... me. It felt as if they were treating the place like a penny peep show, the nosy bastards.

My close neighbours were just brilliant to me though; they kept themselves to themselves, and sometimes they would mark my card if anything was out of place, a bit 'iffy' or suspicious. But you always get one neighbour, don't you, the one who can't mind his own business, wanting to know everything that's going on. I remember one particular neighbour well; he lived at the end of the road. He was about sixty and wore glasses, a little runt of a man. He was always outside his house cleaning his little old car. If he happened to stop you when you were passing his house it was murder, you just couldn't get away from him, he would go on and on; believe me, this fella could talk the leg off a fuckin' donkey.

The very day the 'FOR SALE' sign went up outside my house, literally, only ten minutes had passed when there was a knock on my door. And who should it be? The nosy neighbour! I opened my door and there he was standing there with his 'bins' (glasses) on, smiling.

'All right, Charlie lad,' he said. 'Are you leaving us then?'

I got right on to what this little 'Nosy Parker' was up to; he was dying to see the inside of my house before I left. He knew my background, everybody did, and he wanted to see 'where it had all happened'. I couldn't believe his audacity, treating my home like a house of horrors, like a glorified tourist attraction; the house where my family and I had once shared so many happy memories.

I never let strangers inside my home, only family and close friends, no outsiders whatsoever, but the look on the little prick's face was something else. He wasn't even looking at me properly; his eyes kept jumping past me as he struggled to see into the house. He kept nudging his glasses up his nose to get a better look and would stammer and pause mid-sentence to buy time, so he could stand there longer. Well, I started buzzing off this and I just couldn't resist.

'Would you like to come in for a minute?' I asked him.

He couldn't believe his luck, his eyes bulged and he was through the front door like a shot. I closed the door and began to walk through the hallway towards the kitchen. He was like a shadow; he was that close behind me, inspecting every detail of my home.

'Nice place you have here,' he said to me.

But who did he think he was trying to kid? I could read him like a book; his motives were as transparent as his glasses. He had come to my house; my home; to ogle at me, and he was too fuckin' stupid to think I hadn't got onto him.

Once in the kitchen, he got really excited. I pulled a chair away from the table and invited him to sit down. I then sat opposite him, watching him. All the while he was blabbering on about some rubbish, I can't remember what; I don't think he was even listening to himself. I just sat there and let him get it out, peering into every crevice of the room as he did so, until eventually he said what I was waiting for all along and what he had been itching to say, 'Charlie, is this... where it all happened? You know... right here in the kitchen?'

I watched him as he spoke and carried on watching him even when he finished. I didn't move my gaze for a full minute; he just sat staring back, paralysed by fascination and fear. I waited until he started trembling then I said coldly and quietly, 'See that chair you're sitting on?'

He looked slowly down at the chair then looked up at my eyes, gulped and nodded.

'That was the chair he was sitting on when he was... executed.'

I've never seen anyone move as quickly as he leapt off that chair.

'Oh my God, look at the time, Charlie,' he said, without looking at the clock. 'You'll have to excuse me, I forgot that I promised my wife I'd get the shopping.'

Mopping his brow as he went, he scurried back down the hall and was off down the road in no time, white as a sheet. He glanced back as he went and I just stared at him, unflinching.

When he was gone, I went back inside and closed the door, and nearly pissed myself laughing. Funnily enough, I never did see him again after that little incident; he must have been giving me a wide berth. I wonder why?

As funny as this was, I still anticipated having problems selling the house for exactly that reason. Before it went on the market, a mate called Alan was going to buy it, but his young wife objected because of all that had gone on in it and he gave it a miss. You can't blame them really; even if you aren't bothered, local people know and it can be hard for kids to deal with the stigma. I decided it would probably have to be someone from outside the area, who had never heard of me or the house, and didn't know what had happened. It was, after all, a desirable property, detached in a nice residential area and its own heated swimming pool. Who knows? I thought, Some joker might come along and snap it up. And that's exactly what happened.

At the end of that first day on the market, a load of punters started arriving. What was even stranger was that they were mostly locals. I remember the first guy who arrived, a big shaven headed fella in a brand-new Mercedes, who acted like he knew me from the off, saying, 'All right, Charlie, take the sign down. I'll pay you whenever you want.'

But with all the interest, the price kept going up and up. Eventually, a local couple, who seemed dead genuine and keen, made me an offer I couldn't refuse and I was made up. Little did I know the grief and headaches they would cause me. I certainly didn't expect it to be as stressful as it was; waiting for reports and legal formalities to be done was doing my head in! Once it was eventually finalised, it felt like a big weight off my shoulders and my mind. I remember they came to see the place two days before I was due to move out; no doubt about it, she was the one wearing the trousers out of the two of them.

'Don't forget, Charlie,' she said to me, 'we need you to be set for Friday and out of here by 10:00am.'

I'll never forget that Friday and what went on that day. I was up and packed early; I only had a few suitcases. The furniture had gone the day before so I was all ready for 10:00am as agreed. But 11.00am came and still no sign of them. I called them and there was no answer. Then midday came without a peep. I was doing my nut. I was thinking I had been gazumped somehow and was calling them everything under the sun. Eventually it reached 2.00pm with still no word. I knew then that they had had second thoughts. I thought the offer was too good to be true and the same had happened to them. They had found out that their dream house was once the scene of a murder. Eventually, the man turned up on his own, looking dishevelled and worried. I waited for what was coming.

'Sorry I'm late,' he said. 'I've got a bit of bad news. She doesn't want it,' referring to his wife. I think he probably felt the same way but was using her as his excuse.

'Why did you both leave it this late?' I said. 'I'm all packed up now. I've moved my furniture out. You can't back out this late.'

He just stared at the ground looking miserable. Just then the phone rang. It was my solicitor who had dealt with the sale. I shouted down the phone that I was fuckin' cheesed off with what was happening and he calmed me down and made me explain what had just happened. Then he told me the glorious news. The deal was done; they had tried to stop their solicitor sending the cheque but the secretary had already done it. My solicitor was holding their cheque in his hand.

I couldn't believe what I was hearing and asked him to repeat it. I was so paranoid I asked him to confirm to me that he was definitely a million per cent sure it was through, and he just said it was and to take it easy. I put the phone down and looked at the new owner of my house, still staring sheepishly at the floor. My conversation with the solicitor had been exciting and stressful for me, but I had never let slip the good news. To him, it sounded like I was getting confirmation of the bad news.

'I'm sorry,' he said.

'So am I,' I replied. 'But don't worry, no hard feelings. Anyway I've got a present for you.'

I walked over to the front door and took the keys out of the lock.

I handed them to him.

'The house is yours now, lad. Oh, and by the way, I won't charge you for the ghost. You can have that for free.'

I then picked up my cases and walked out of that house for the very last time, leaving behind me all the secrets and memories, secrets never to be told; secrets that will die with me. Somehow, I felt free again to concentrate on the plans I had for the future. I was ready to start a new beginning.

First, though I had to get myself some decent living accommodation. After all, I am now on my own since my family have grown up and gone their separate ways, and though I had somewhere temporary to stay, it was far from ideal. I was toying with the idea of living right in the heart of Liverpool city centre, since there are some tidy apartments for sale there. I have good friends in the property business so I would have had no problems price-wise if I were to buy one. Liverpool city centre is a fantastic place to live nowadays; it has all the amenities one could ever wish for and a person could never get bored or lonely living there. There is only one problem; the Liverpool lifestyle that goes with it. Don't get me wrong, the lifestyle is just too good to be true - the bars, the nightclubs and the women! Well, they're just something else, young and beautiful, in fact the majority of Scouse birds are.

The nightlife in our city is fantastic. I usually hit the bars and clubs about twice a week, but if I lived next to them I think the temptation would be too much. I would never get anything done; I'd be partying every night and sleeping all day. How long could I keep that hectic pace up for? God only knows. I had to sack the idea off; a pad in the city centre just wouldn't work for me. I needed somewhere a bit more tranquil, somewhere I could chill out and think. I knew something would turn up for me. It always does.

A few weeks later, I was visiting a place called Knowsley, a few miles outside Liverpool. I had been on a meet with a couple of mates and, after we had finished business, I began to head back towards Liverpool and, as luck would have it, though I didn't realise it at the time, I was deep in thought and took the wrong turning on the motorway. It was such a warm summer's afternoon that I didn't even notice at first, I was enjoying the ride that much, but I found as I watched out for a turning that I began to get a warm feeling inside that I usually get when something good is about to happen. It's like a sixth sense I have had since I was a kid, the kind of thing that makes people say, 'I feel lucky today'.

I was dead relaxed and was driving a lot slower than I normally do, in fact so slowly that it was making other drivers irate. But I just knew I had to take my time for some reason. So I thought, Fuck them, let them keep beeping if they want to. I was just following the bonnet of my car, without a care in the world. Before long, I was deep in the rural countryside about fifteen miles outside Liverpool. As I was driving, I spotted a sign saying: Rainford Village, and it pointed me down quite a narrow country road. I don't know why but I just followed it; it was beckoning me to.

As I drove, I was certain I had been down that lane before, every bend was familiar. Then it came back to me. I had been there nearly fifty years earlier with a mate called Joey Hannigan.

When we were ten or eleven, we were always sagging school together and would ride our stolen bikes; which were heavily disguised, into fields looking for apples to steal, and anything else we could get our hands on in the farms we came across. After all, we were just two street kids from Liverpool living on our wits all those years ago. These memories filled my mind as I rounded the last bend and entered Rainford Village itself.

I parked up and climbed out to have a stroll around, remarking at the total lack of any parking meters. I looked up the road and saw something I had not seen in a long while. An old lady was being escorted across the road by two teenage lads, one with a David Beckham haircut. I just thought to myself, You wouldn't see that in the inner city; I thought those manners were long gone, but the whole village had that kind of an air. People were cheerful and they would say 'Hello' as you passed them in the street.

Just as I stepped out into the street, I got another shock from times long ago. The sweet shop, I recognised it from many years before; 1952 to be precise. Joey and I had wandered into this village and had ended up in all sorts of trouble. It all started in that shop, where I had robbed a bar of chocolate and a comic and Joey had whizzed a handful of sugared barley sticks. We had the goodies stuffed into our pockets but the owner soon got on to us; we must have stood out like a sore thumb, two little Scouse kids robbing his shop. We legged it and before we knew it he was on our tail. We jumped on the bikes and peddled like fuck, all the while the shopkeeper yelling at passers-by to stop us.

Some of them decided to help him and, before long, it felt like the whole village was part of the chase. We were laughing as we rode until I turned round and saw a massive copper on to us, chasing us on his bike, going like the clappers. My bottle just went as he came out of nowhere, blowing his whistle and pedalling after us with all his might. You would have thought we had done a massive armed bank robbery the way everyone was carrying on! But we were younger and faster and we found a narrow dirt road coming off the main road out of the village, which we sped down.

Halfway down this track we found a big cornfield, and spread out across it were literally hundreds of little haystacks shaped like Indian wigwams. I shouted to Joey that we should hide in there and he agreed, but as we turned, I pulled on my brakes a bit too hard and flew over the handlebars and into the fence post, breaking my front tooth in half. It still has a cap on it today, a war wound from that robbery all those years ago.

We threw our bikes down and covered them with hay and then ducked behind one of the little haystacks. We waited there for what seemed like a few hours, keeping our eyes peeled for bizzies, me with blood all over my shirt and face, but eventually we realised they had given up the ghost so we both got off home, safe and sound, eager to enjoy our 'stolen goods' in comfort.

As I walked down the street on that summer afternoon in August 2002, it was hard to believe 50 years had passed since my school mate Joey and I had evaded capture by what seemed like half the people of Rainford village; a chase that will remain etched on my memory for ever.

I found an olde-worlde-style tea room where I ordered a pot of tea, happy just sitting watching the world go by. However, the building opposite caught my eye and soon I found I was looking it over. It was tall and the upper half was obviously residential; it had clean white walls and long Georgian windows, with window baskets full of flowers, and even had a beech tree providing a bit of seclusion. As I inspected it, I saw the 'for sale' sign, and before long, it was enticing me to go and take a closer look.

I wanted to know the price, my guess was in the region of two hundred and fifty to three hundred grand for a building that size in Liverpool, or at least a million in London. I gulped my tea down and went straight over to take a look. Luckily, the owners were in, and were nice enough, offering to let me take a look around. I was amazed at the size of the place; three double bedrooms, one of which was en suite, and a large lounge, bathroom and kitchen and so on. But the best part was when they invited me to see the back. The garden was incredible; ornate flowerbeds backed on to woodland, filled with wild birds and rabbits, with a large lawn to the side. There was even an outbuilding with a Spanish patio. For me, it was heaven. I couldn't contain my excitement and I made the couple an offer there and then on the spot. I wanted to buy it right away, and when I found out how reasonable it was, eventually I did. I am still doing work on the place though; there is a lot to be done, especially with the alarms and cameras I needed. You can't be too careful when you've got a history like mine.

But my life here is exactly what I always wanted. It is so different to the city; each morning I awake to the sound of birds, and open my blinds to the view of the garden and the fields and countryside beyond. Then from the front I can see the hustle and bustle of the village as it awakes each morning. It's a nice change, back to old-fashioned values. I know quite a lot of people round the village and occasionally someone will recognise me, or kids will come up and say they've seen me on the TV or their parents have read my books. People want to know though; with it being a close-knit community, what makes someone like me move there? And they ask all sorts of questions. I just like to keep a low profile, though sometimes it's impossible. People are friendly and they invite you to local events, but like I say, I keep myself to myself.

When I do happen to go on a bender, out partying, I head back to Liverpool. I am so close that I never get lonely with friends just a few miles away. The best cure that I can find for loneliness, though, is a beautiful woman. I love women; what man doesn't? I always give women respect because they deserve it.

Most men, compared with women, are weak and selfish in many ways. I know villains who are big, hard men, but are terrified of their wives or girlfriends, especially if they have been out the night before and particularly if they have copped off with another girl. I have met many a pal of mine, men who have been on armed robberies with me, or some other heavy work and these same people are petrified of going home to face their wives after being out all night. I have done it myself; I have actually brought a couple of pals home with me to our house the morning after being out all night, having done a bit of business. I have found that one of the hardest things to do is to front up to your wife or girlfriend.

Women can't be fooled; men think they are fooling them but Liverpool women, especially, are too 'wide'. They have this uncanny way of finding out if you have been with another woman; even if it comes down to finding a hair on your clothes, or a trace of make-up, or even a smell. They know, all right!

I remember coming home late one night thinking I was clever. Whenever I went out and ended up with a bit of strange, I always kept a change of clothes in the boot of my car. This particular night, I was changing back into the clothes I had left home in that evening. I was at the side of the road with my boot open putting on my original clothes when, all of a sudden, a cop car pulled up next to me. I had a lot of explaining to do. I had to explain why, at 4.00am, I was changing my clothes. After listening to my explanation, the dirty bastards phoned my house and told my wife. I had to face it all when I got home.

I find that most women are good judges of character when it comes to seeing through your friends or mates. The best judge is usually your mother, who can sense if your so-called friend is good or bad. My mother would sometimes say to me, 'Charlie, that mate of yours, there's something about him which doesn't seem right.'

And I would always defend them, saying, 'Don't worry, Mam, he's alright.'

But most of the time her words would ring true. The same went for my wife. She would meet a certain mate of mine and tell me that he was false and not a true friend.

Looking back, most women I have known have been right in their judgements. There is the old saying, 'Never trust a woman'...

well, I have put a lot of trust in some of the women I have known. I believe that if a woman loves and trusts a man, she would be willing to die for him. Providing he is truthful and not a liar, she will forgive him for most of the crimes he has committed, even murder. When it comes to her other half playing around though, that is unforgivable!

The only problem is; they come and go with me these days, which I suppose is down to me. When a woman gets a bit too close, I sort of switch off, I have to. More so if she is decent and respectable; I hate the idea of my stigma sticking to them. I don't want my past to lead them into jeopardy and I always try to be truthful, since there is nothing more hurtful to a woman than deceit. There are times I feel that without the love of one of God's greatest creations; a woman, life is just not worth living!

CHAPTER 15

I recently received information that one of the dogs involved in my kidnapping was seen coming and going frequently from a house in the Wavertree area of Liverpool. I did not yet know whether the information was reliable or not, but whenever I hear the possible whereabouts of any of them, I have to follow it up. There have been many sightings of these hyenas that I have had to get used to, many leads ending up being wild goose chases, and you save a lot of time if you learn to sniff out good information from bad. It takes a long time, years in fact, but nevertheless my burning hatred for these animals drives me on.

I will hunt this scum down even if it takes me until the day I die.

On this occasion, I decided to drive into the city to check out the information and, although I didn't expect anything big, I was well pumped up with adrenalin. I was meeting these two young, dead game kids; family, and close to me blood-wise. My plan was to sit off and make sure the details were bang on before any steps were taken. Sightings of this scum have got back to me from all over the planet: Spain, the Dam (Holland), even Turkey. But more often than not, leads are old by the time they are pursued and the trail goes cold.

After speaking to the kids and verifying that the information was probably good, the three of us drove to the house. When we arrived, the fella who had marked our card came out from where he had been keeping watch and told us we had just missed the dog. Somehow, he had got a sniff that we were on our way there and had done one. How he had got on to us, fuck knows. Although the card marker was a good lad whom I know quite well, I still have my doubts with people these days.

'I hope to fuck you're not having me on!' I said to him. 'This wouldn't be a wind-up would it?'

'Charlie,' he replied, 'honest to God, he was definitely here but he's fucked off. I swear. I saw him leave the gaff about ten minutes ago.'

I couldn't be arsed asking him which way he'd gone or what motor he was in or anything, I was too busy wondering who else this fella had told about this. Some fellas just can't hold their own water and it was a good job nothing happened; it's too dangerous taking chances with outsiders being on the scene. So I just said to him, 'Yeah, all right. Just leave it,' and got back into our car and drove off.

It was 3.00am and there was no way I was going to put us on offer driving around the city at that time in the morning.

I got the two kids to drop me where I'd left my car and, as they drove away, I walked over to my motor and noticed a dead suspicious car parked a little way away with two fellas in it. I got into my motor and, as I was driving away, the car I had sussed out behind me started to pull away as well and followed me, keeping its distance the whole time. Whenever I turned it would turn with me. I know the city centre of Liverpool like the back of my hand so I decided to head for some back streets and try to lose them. I put a bit of distance between us and, when they were out of sight, I parked and ran dead fast to a doorway where I could position myself in a shadow but still see all that went on. I was only just in the doorway when the other car screeched to a halt behind my motor. I stayed put and watched closely what was happening.

I was all tensed up. I had no idea who the fuck they were and I wasn't even tooled up; I had nothing to defend myself with. The one good thing I had was my vest strapped on me; my body armour. I always wear it when I go out in the city at night; you can never tell, and at that moment I was fully convinced that the two in that car wanted to cop for me. The situation had all the hallmarks of a drive-by shooting.

I weighed up my options. I needed a route away from the

doorway, some way of getting off discreetly in the darkness. But there was none. I had only one choice; to stay and watch them and hope they didn't start searching for me. The two men got out; one was talking on his mobile and the other looking the car over. As they did this, I breathed a huge sigh of relief; the way they moved told me they were obviously bizzies.

They got off pretty quickly in their unmarked car and I waited a while just to be safe, then I did one myself. All the while I was thinking to myself, Why are they on my case? I wondered if they had sussed something out. It's unusual for the police to trail villains by car these days; they don't need to make their presence felt. They can just use a tracking device on the underneath of a villain's car and monitor every move they make. Maybe I should leave all the hard work of capturing the animal to them, but if they are depending on me for leads, then I don't think they should hold their breath. Besides, when you have a burning revenge inside you, it's hard to let go.

I was wrapped up in these thoughts when I arrived home and, when I opened my front door, I saw a note had been pushed through my letter box. It was from the police saying they wanted to speak to me regarding a very serious matter. Well, they could just keep on wanting for all I cared; I could do without them hounding me. I had had enough of their surveillance when I lived in Liverpool, but now, in this beautiful, tranquil little village, I didn't want them knocking on my door every five minutes.

I finally turned in for what was left of the night and dropped off at about 5.00am after tossing and turning. After having only a couple of hours' sleep, I was awoken by the sound of my front door being hammered on. It was the police. Who else? Only this time, it was the Liverpool Murder Squad.

Once a villain gets a violent reputation, it never goes away. Unfortunately, that is exactly what has happened to me over the years, mostly from incidents in my younger days. I never wanted a reputation and certainly never went out of my way to get one. With everything I have done in my criminal past, I have always tried to keep a low profile but some people just won't let that happen, least of all the police. Rumours get spread and events get exaggerated until it becomes ridiculous. Some villains will go to extremes to try to get themselves a reputation, while some want to be recognised and in the limelight. Others just want names as hard-cases to be able to go out of their way to intimidate people; they are usually bullies and are mostly despised.

Unfortunately for me, the harder I try to avoid a reputation the more one sticks to me, and so, in this instance, the police decided to interview me over a recent murder in Liverpool. Why me? Not because of reliable information or a witness statement, but because of my past criminal life. It was their usual interview routine; where was I at the time? Did I ever visit the area where the shooting took place? Did I know him? And so it went on. I wasn't being funny with them, I just started answering their questions to the best of my abilities. After all, we do have to have some sort of law and order and they have got their job to do.

But like most bizzies these days, they were getting nowhere and this was looking just like all the other unsolved murders carried out in Liverpool in the last five years. As I have mentioned before, murder is a common occurrence in our cities these days; not a week goes by without somebody being shot dead. We all know most of these killings are carried out amongst the criminal fraternity, but nevertheless, these sorts of killings are on the increase. Most of today's villains think, and some even know, they can get away with murder, and the saying is becoming a reality. Some young villains know that as long as the necessary precautions are taken, it can be done. Taking precautions such as no witnesses who can identify them, no forensics (DNA evidence), no obvious motive and a good, strong alibi. Of course, the most valuable tool can be yourself and your composure, like how you stand up under a strong grilling and how you handle yourself in front of the Murder Squad. If a shooter checks all those points, the chances are pretty slim of him getting charged. The rest is down to the individual and the aftermath; can your conscience hold out? Can you live with the secret of knowing you have taken the life of another human being for the rest of your days?

Some villains have to tell somebody, they just can't hold it in. But what if you have a fall-out with a person you told, someone you trusted who now holds your life in their hands. Keeping yourself together in the aftermath; the days, months and years that follow something like that is the real test. The Murder Squad deal with murders and murderers all day every day and they are not stupid. They have been trained and, although it's difficult to pin you down without sufficient evidence, they can hassle you and make your life a misery. You have to have real strength to withstand that.

And that was what I was getting here. I was asked endless questions as they tried to suss me out about a shooting that had nothing whatsoever to do with me, something that was becoming increasingly obvious. One of the investigating officers was a woman.

'Charlie,' she said to me, 'this is a senseless killing. The man who has been shot dead was just an ordinary fella. He had no criminal record or connections. He was a clean-living, family man. We are puzzled why anybody would want to kill him.'

'Why have you come to see me?' I asked her. 'You know quite well I haven't been involved with this in any sort of way.'

I was then told someone had put my name forward and they are obliged to follow up any leads they receive. In other words, some dirty bastard had decided to make life difficult for me. I was a bit puzzled by what she'd told me, especially when I found out that the victim was a family man with no connections. If he actually was all the things she said he was, what was he doing socialising in a pub notorious for violence and full of villains from every walk of life? It was witnessed that the killer knew who he was after and walked straight over to him. I just can't see why someone would do that to a stranger. The killer had reputedly called him names beforehand, like, 'You dirty bastard,' and in my opinion, there was a lot more to it than the police knew.

After the interview, the policewoman said, 'We had to eliminate you from the investigation, Charlie. You know the score.'

'Yeah, yeah all right,' I replied, 'just don't be pulling up outside my premises and making it plain obvious for all to see.'

But the bizzies don't care about any embarrassment they cause you, so it was like talking to a brick wall. I am the one with the reputation from the past and it will never leave me, no matter how hard I try. I just hope the bizzies don't start hounding me again now I have adjusted to village life.

Weeks had gone by since that police incident and I thought everything was back to normal until I found out that the London press were on my case. I pulled up outside my house and there they were, waiting for me. I shouted to them, 'What do you lot want? What's all this about?'.

A man approached me and said they had come up from London and asked if he could have a word. I didn't want a scene outside my home and people were starting to stop and look at what was going on. I told him he had better come in, but to get shut of the photographer. The reporter looked a bit apprehensive at first, but eventually agreed. When I think about it, some of these journalists have got some bottle; after all, they don't know what they're getting themselves into or what to expect from villains with notorious backgrounds. As he showed me respect and manners, I put him at ease when we got inside.

'All right, what's this all about? I asked. 'Who put you on to me?'

He then spilled everything out. It became apparent that the newspaper he was working for were doing a big investigation on a top Premiership footballer; England international and captain of Liverpool, Steven Gerrard. The young footballer, who is a world class player, had allegedly been getting the frighteners put on him by a young Liverpool villain.

The threats of violence were getting so bad that it was starting to affect Gerrard's playing. He was well-known as a good, clean-living kid, a thorough gentleman and not involved with violence, the criminal world, or gangsters in any way.

All this pressure on the kid meant his career was starting to suffer; thinking he's doing the right thing, he goes to the police for protection from this violent bully. But the police offer nothing, saying as usual that they had no evidence to go on. What could he do? Who could he turn to? He was stuck between the devil and the deep blue sea. Eventually, someone must have done him a big favour without him knowing about it. The bully came unstuck, as they all do eventually and ended up in a right mess. He got a right working-over; his jaw was wired up and he was even shot in the mouth.

Who did it? I wouldn't know and, to be quite frank, I don't want to know, but obviously there are other people who want to know, like this news reporter who came all the way from London to see me. It turned out that I was supposed to have been the one who sorted out the villain who terrorised the young footballer. Well, I want to make one thing quite clear here for the record; I had absolutely nothing at all to do with that nonsense. I asked the news reporter where he got his information from, but he wouldn't reveal anything to me, for obvious reasons.

'Whoever told you I had something to do with this told you a pack of lies,' I retorted, 'and better still, you should go and get your few quid back off the prick.'

Nevertheless, a few days later in February 2003, the whole story was splashed all over the national papers, my name included, saying I had been charged with the murder of this young villain's father in 1998 but was found not guilty. Why they had to go and drag all that up and put it in the papers after all these years is beyond me.

A few months after the police visit, the same young villain was charged with selling Class A drugs. He was found guilty and copped out for a few years. A Liverpool police officer who was charged with a series of corruption offences, and is now awaiting trial, has been publicly accused of having worked together with this villain.

It's funny, don't you think, because a few years earlier when I stood in the High Court accused of the murder of this villain's father, there was a police officer present, a friend of the deceased, who was also charged with corruption alongside this first officer. This officer had stolen sensitive documents from intelligence headquarters, including a three-page document containing vital evidence relating to my trial. This same police officer not only admitted to the theft of these vital documents but had also conspired along with three other people. If that is not perverting the course of justice, then what is?

When this policeman did finally go to trial over stealing this sensitive document, and the evidence was overwhelming, what do you think the outcome of this trial was? Fuck all! He didn't even lose his job or get suspended from duty. The reason? The trial judge said it would not be in the public interest to continue with this case and he walked out of the court a free man, so where is the justice? The bizzie's name was Sgt Mark Kevin Davies... enough said.

I will never forget that day in court when it all came out about the police corruption. The judge went haywire and I am certain it was one of the main reasons the jury acquitted me. Without that bizzie getting exposed, my trial could have gone the other way and I would now be serving life. This seems like history repeating itself, or 'Like father, like son,' as they say; both of them working with bent bizzies.

Many years ago, when my friends were young villains and involved with our type of crime, we made our views quite clear to one another. We were always on one side of the fence and they were on the other. You couldn't be on both sides; you couldn't run with the hare and the hounds. They were our rules, rules that were never broken, and not one of us would have dreamed of working alongside a bizzie, no way. We would sooner have died than broken the code, and that just isn't the case anymore with some young street villains. Rules held me and my mates together in those days; nowadays some younger villains don't have rules. I am not saying all, but some are lazy and greedy, value drugs and money more than friends and family, and when drugs become more important than people you end up with anarchy.

I would like to think most people in this country are aware of the drug problem that underlies a lot of crime in our cities, but is it the cause of violent crime and murder? Has it created the lowlife mugger who beats and rapes and harms young and old alike? Does it create the scum who would steal from their mother and sell his soul for a fix? And is it responsible for the hyenas and their kind who have moved up the ladder from exactly these kinds of beginning to commit kidnappings and murders fuelled by drugs? And are drugs responsible for girls becoming drug addicts and then turning to prostitution just to get a fix? These girls are past caring and, with heads so fucked up on drugs, they will keep taking the risks just to put a needle in their arm.

So are drugs to blame for all of this? It is, like so many things, not a simple case of yes or no, because drug addicts and users aren't always at the bottom of the pile, there are plenty at the top of it as well. I am referring to your seemingly clean, upright young citizens of today. I have been to the parties and mingled with celebrities, actors, writers, lawyers, football stars and many other VIPs and, believe me, once these parties are in full swing and the 'beak' gets lined up on the table, most of these guests have a dabble at it. There are not too many who abstain.

Just a few weeks ago, I was invited back to some wealthy businessman's house. He was having a big bash and had it all laid on: the best food, wine, a swimming pool, the lot. It was impressive and over a hundred guests were there. Just as things were getting going, he stood up to make a speech. He and his wife were clean-living types and anti-drugs.

'If there's anybody here who takes drugs,' he stated, 'or has drugs on them, will they please leave now. I won't allow it in my house.'

And what do you think happened? Nearly everybody walked out of the house; the place was nearly empty within a couple of minutes. Most of those people who had left were your clean-cut, respectable types but deep down they were all at it and into drugs. They are not all that different from your street mugger or prostitute. They only difference is they don't have to go out and mug anybody or go on the game to buy their drugs because they are fortunate enough to already have the money from good work or other sources.

Paul Getty Jr was one of the wealthiest men in the world and a self-confessed heroin addict. Underneath all his money and status, he was still just another smack-head. Two years ago, I sat on the panel of a live TV talk show, whose other guests included Howard Marks, author or *Mr Nice,* and Jimmy McGovern. A mate of mine, Ged Keogh, was sitting in the audience. I was asked by some members of the audience what my views were on the drug situation, and one of the people who asked was a major TV star who had recently played the role of a heroin addict on television. I said to them, 'In my opinion, all drugs in this country should be legalised.' The audience went wild and clapped like mad in agreement and Jimmy McGovern nodded to me in approval. I then gave my reasons.

'First of all, it would help reduce violent muggings, because we all know that when a smack-head gets those cravings they will stop at nothing for a fix. Second, the other crowd who are right at the top of the ladder would be put right out of business and wouldn't be back-stabbing and ripping one another off, helping to end the wars that always end in bloodshed, and mothers losing their sons and daughters, making violent crime and murder a lot less frequent than they are now.'

I am not a politically-minded person, but every Government elected in this country in recent times has kept pretending it will all go away, and don't seem to have realised how serious it has become. But, then again, they don't live in the real world, or they pretend they don't. I would like to see their reactions and how they would cope if they were to live on one of these council estates amongst it all.

There is a hell of a lot of turmoil in this country and people young and old are being intimidated. It's all very well for some of these politicians laying the rules down saying you must live side by side in harmony with one another. That's all right for them, they don't have to live in a deprived area where the only rule that counts is dog eat dog. If drugs were legalised, or at least dealt with properly, I am almost certain it would turn everything around for the better.

If there were drug centres in every town and city, that were properly controlled in the right way by the Government and their officials, that would mean any smack-head, crack-head or any other addict could walk into one of those drug centres and be given whatever treatment and advice they needed for free. He or she would know they wouldn't have to steal or mug anybody for their craving and we might see the start of cutting down on that sick crime. By doing this, it would save millions in tax-payers' money, it would help us to ease the congested prison system and take pressure off government officials trying to control an out-of-control situation.

Another potential effect of the legalisation of drugs is that when people know they can have something cheaply or easily, they sort of shy away from it. It has a sort of psychological effect on people and you could possibly get that situation where 'you can't even give the goods away, nobody wants them'. With the buzz and mystique taken away from them, especially for the respectable and rich, who spend a fortune on cocaine, drugs could lose their glamour and appeal. And you'd probably also see the majority of them giving the drugs scene up because they wouldn't want to be classed in the same category as the lowlife.

I remember when some mates of mine and I had just left school in 1956. We were all about the same age, fifteen or sixteen years old. There were no drugs around then; you just never came across them. We were all clean kids, like most teenagers in the 1950s. The only vice we had was the odd ciggie or pint of beer. The ciggies were easy to get hold of but trying to buy a pint of beer in an alehouse was sometimes dead hard. After all, we were only young lads and some of us didn't even shave. We looked like what we were... kids. But we would go into the pub and stick our chest out, stand on our toes a little bit and just hope the landlord took us for eighteen and served us.

When I did get lucky and was served, I noticed something in those pubs 45 years ago, something that made me open my eyes and want to vomit. We would see old women, some with shawls over their shoulders, and old-looking men, wearing flat caps and thick buckled leather belts. We would see most of them passing little miniature boxes to one another, dipping their fingers in, pinching some brown powder out and sniffing it like mad up their noses. It was a horrible sight; all their nostrils were an orange-brown colour and it used to make me sick, especially the snorting noise they would make for ages afterwards. They were using snuff, a substance made from tobacco ground to a fine powder, and it is one of the most addictive drugs on this planet, a rival even to cocaine or heroin.

When a heroin or cocaine addict goes into rehab, the drugs are out of their system in weeks. This is not the case with snuff; the nicotine is even more powerful and deadly and, for smokers who give up, it takes years for the last of it to go. They are often lucky if the craving goes away at all. These old men and women I saw all those years ago snorting that deadly tobacco poison up their noses were doing something completely legal and something that had been done for centuries by the aristocracy in the country, who would carry their snuff in expensive silver or gold snuff boxes, some with their names engraved on them. I know about this because I have had quite a few of these expensive little snuff boxes away when I was in the light removal business! Of course, the poor man in the street couldn't afford those expensive items; he had to make do with a little old tin box. But this was all legal, and tobacco will always be legal as it makes billions for the government in tax.

Thinking back to when I was being tortured by those hyenas, strapped to a chair in Airey's filthy house for two days, I imagine how I could have ended up if I had refused to make that phone call to my brother. Those animals were deadly serious when they were going to inject me with heroin. One of them wanted to cut my eyes out. If they had kept me a few days longer and kept plugging me with heroin, I could easily have ended up a smackhead, maybe a blind one at that.

Something needs to be done about the drug situation in this country, and soon. Despite our technology, despite our successes and our culture, drug addiction is on the increase and in my opinion, it should be properly controlled. Of course, there are people who take drugs but it is control that determines why some use them and others just abuse them. It doesn't take a genius to see that this country, along with today's modern morality, is beginning to display all the hallmarks of the fall of the Roman Empire.

EPILOGUE

Today, as I write this last chapter of that ordeal of mine; when I was cunningly tricked by that lowlife degenerate Lea, I will never forget walking into that filthy den where the rest of those animals were lying in wait for me. I can still see their faces laughing and screaming while they carried out their torture on me using their guns, knives and their teeth like the dogs they are.

I can still see the face of Lea as he poured the boiling water on to parts of my body; badly scalding me. I can still remember him shouting to the others who had me held down, 'Fuckin' turn him over!' But they couldn't turn me over. I had held on to what strength I had left in me. And I can still remember Lea starting to scream in frustration, 'Drag his fuckin' kecks down, I'm gonna burn his dick off!'

That sick bastard wanted to take my manhood away from me. I can still remember the gun pressed hard against my head waiting for the bullet to enter my brain. I can still remember everything. Over the years, I have faced death many times but nowhere near as close as that last time. There are some memories in a person's life that can never be erased. I can never forget and I can never forgive.

Is it any wonder I start to feel this familiar, burning hatred erupting inside of me? It is only then that I start to really go on one. Sometimes, my family and friends see me in this way and they try their best to console me. 'Take it easy,' they tell me. 'It will soon be sorted.' 'Time will tell.' But will I have enough time? Will I have enough time to wait and take out my revenge on these animals? I don't know. I don't want to still be hunting those dogs when a few more years have passed me by. Of course, at the present, my hands are tied because two of these scum are still inside, so copping for them is out of the question, although I have heard from good friends of mine that that pair have been dealt with while they have been doing their sentences. Perhaps they have been upsetting the wrong people in prison.

As for the rest of the pack, the last update I heard was that they were living abroad somewhere. All this becomes so frustrating to me at times but I know there is little I can do at the moment. I will just have to bide my time and wait, and above all, keep tight control of my patience. I have always been a person who takes great care with my self-discipline, particularly in the past when I would plan and organise most of the graft my friends and I were about to take part in, and more so if they were heavy armed blags.

As I look back on all of this, it only seems like yesterday I was out with staunch friends, good men with decency and honour, on a job. I always made double-sure before we raided any of those security vans, banks, mail sorting offices or whatever that everything looked right. For example, if there was something we had overlooked, something that should not have been there, no matter how trivial it might have seemed, I would insist we call the whole operation off. Sometimes, but not too often, one of the boys would say to me, 'Charlie, what's wrong? We can do it, everything looks OK.'

But I would always keep my control and not get erratic. I knew deep down we were all dead game and we had plenty of bottle, but it only took one small amount of madness, to fuck things up big time; if we ignored the good instincts we relied on, in an instant it could be 'God help us all.' We would probably end up serving a lifetime of long, lonely years behind prison bars. I remember one such piece of graft we were about to have off. It was a big national colliery situated a few miles outside Liverpool and employing a couple of thousand men, according to our information. You can imagine the amount of cash flow on the premises. We had been doing our homework on this coal mine for weeks, going over and over our plans meticulously, inch by inch. When the day finally came to have it away, just two hours before we were ready to go into the place, I asked two mates to come with me to take one last look, making sure everything was still sound. It was only a fifteen-minute drive from Liverpool at the most.

When we arrived, we pulled the motor up a little distance away from the building where the money was held. We noticed that next to the doors at the entrance, the very doors we had spent weeks planning to steam into, for some inexplicable reason a garden shed had been erected. I said to my mates that it shouldn't be there, and that it hadn't been there when we had last come to look. I took one of my friends over with me for a closer look.

There was plenty of activity taking place around that time; the workers were changing their shifts and we both went over to take a look wearing miners' clothes and helmets. The garden shed had a window; and as we walked past I glanced into it to see two or three people sitting low inside. I got a terrible feeling about it all. I was certain they were bizzies, who else could they be? They were definitely not coal miners, or landscape gardeners that was for sure. We decided to cancel the whole job and were later proved to have done the right thing when we received good information that the police had been waiting in ambush in the shed, with more of them hidden elsewhere... all armed!

The reason I mention that incident from years ago is because, in the past, I did live a life of crime. I was no angel and I will admit I was an out-and-out villain, as were many of my friends, and I'm not going to make excuses for what I was. But there was a vast difference in the way my friends and I approached the crimes we committed, as opposed to what the scum of today get up to. We were men of honour and decency. We never went around harming innocent people or mugging old men and women for their pensions. Those types of criminals were totally despicable to our crowd and still are.

I know this doesn't give me the right to go out and do what I did in order to get money. In those bygone days, I don't think the crimes we committed affected anyone too severely; after all, we only stole from those who could afford to lose a bit of their wealth, such as the rich fat cats and their companies. They were the ones we targeted, not the ordinary working-class man or woman. I know this is a controversial standpoint, and that there are some victims of crime who would find this difficult to come to terms with, but I am steadfast in my views and always will be.

One day, I was browsing through the local newspaper and stumbled on an article about me sent in by a local reader. It urged the people or Merseyside to boycott *'Killer'*, written by Charlie Seiga, a 'known gangster'. It was written by a local woman named Joan Jonker, who, I'm sure, would be disappointed to discover how significantly her letter boosted the sales of my book. She heads a Victims of Crime support group, and apparently did not know that, just before writing her letter, I had donated my entire Criminal Injuries Award to women and kids at the mercy of the scum in this city, a good few grand that her organisation gladly accepted from this 'known gangster'. I still have a letter from them thanking me. I'm sure that if she ever becomes the victim of a serious crime, which I sincerely hope she never does, and this gangster Charlie Seiga came steaming in to save her from a gang of thugs, she might have a change of heart about me! Because that's what my mates and I would do; we would help any man, woman or child in a terrible situation in an instant. The trouble with Joan Jonker and her kind is that they are quick to condemn people before they get the facts right.

Of course, there are some villains who are ruthless and have no compassion, but there are also some young decent villains who have good qualities and would go to the aid of a person if they had to. Loyalty and trust in each other were other sound qualities we possessed, especially if one of our mates came unstuck on a bit of graft we had been doing. The rest of us were confident we could go home and sleep soundly knowing full well we wouldn't be betrayed, and that if that mate of ours happened to get sent down, his family would be looked after by us all. I have two young relatives who are doing this right now. One of their mates came unstuck and got ten years. He and his family get looked after every week without fail. It helps to alleviate the anxiety while serving your sentence.

But there are some people in prison who have nothing and nobody to help them. Take the likes of Lea; I went out of my way to help that vile bastard and look how he repaid me. I'm not just talking about the kidnapping and torture I had to endure, but the way I was betrayed. That rat made those false statements against me to his lawyers for them to read out in court, branding me as a big heroin dealer, going around the city selling drugs to young kids. Not only that; he also made a verbal statement in court saying I had shot a man dead. As I have mentioned previously, if that is not grassing I don't know what is. That is why, in the end, I played that sick bastard at his own game; he was the one who broke the rules not me. I know the conflict against dogs like these will never end. I hate the scum and the lowlife, and as long as I am alive, I always will. I am a man who still retains his honour and dignity.

Writing this book has been like a creative therapy for me. I have found out much about myself in ways I never thought possible. Who would have thought I would have ended up this way? It's still hard to believe that not so long ago I was classed as a ruthless gangster and a killer facing a life sentence for shooting dead a predator who went around this city terrorising ordinary men and women. I know for a fact that according to certain people I will eventually be killed. All I can say to that is, whoever you are, make sure you plan it properly and have the bottle to put one in my head instead of half-heartedly in my leg. If you're going to do the job, do it right. After all, we all have to die sometime, it's just a matter of when and where.

There is one consolation though, whatever the outcome may be, and being the age I have now reached; I cannot die young... but those lowlife scum can!

They say when hyenas have their victims beaten they release a hideous laugh. This may be true, I don't know; I never got the chance to find out. The hyenas had me down, but never beaten. Maybe in the end it will be *me* who has the last laugh!

If you have enjoyed this book, you will love Charlie's interviews on Shaun Attwood's podcast on YouTube, and we appreciate your Amazon reviews.

ABOUT THE AUTHOR

Bestselling author of
Killer, The Hyenas, A Liverpool Streetwise Kid
and **A Killer Vigilante**

In 1952, quote from Charlie: 'My life of crime began after I had a vicious street-fight with another kid. He was the local hard-case bully; he and his gang used to waylay me and my two friends. My friends and I were good little earners at that time, and because they couldn't make anything themselves, the hard case bully used to force us to hand over any gear that we had on us. It was like a sort of mugging that goes on today. He was bigger and older than me; aged 15, but I fronted him up and made a mess of him. That gained me the respect of all the local street kids, and I became a gang leader; I was just 12 years old!'

At the age of thirteen he meets his mentor a woman of thirty-eight years old, her name is Winnie. With Winnie, Charlie progresses further, she has him well-groomed and dressed as an office boy wearing a blazer and shirt and tie and she teaches him how to steal expensive diamond rings from under the noses of high class jewellers. This was well planned out, displaying real classic cases of robberies which were highly rewarding.

In 1954 at the age of fourteen and with his daring young gang they pulled off robberies that would put a professional criminal to shame, and he became one of the richest teenagers in the city of Liverpool, where they operated from.

1955. At fifteen years old he eventually gets caught for a jewel heist and even though he is a juvenile he still gets severely treated and interrogated. Police methods were ruthless in those days. He was taken outside in the freezing cold winter rain and handcuffed to a cast iron drainpipe for hours all because he refused to sign a confessed statement. Eventually he was remanded to a juvenile remand home, where he witnessed the sexual abuse of young boys, by their carers, who liked to be called Master or Sir. Charlie rebelled over what he had seen, and due to the subsequent uproar he caused in the remand home he was finally released on bail and, ironically, all charges against him were dropped.

Quote from Charlie: 'Before arriving at Woolton Vale juvenile remand home, I had heard all kinds of stories from kids on the outside about what went on there. Some of the staff were beasts. At night in the dormitory it would sometimes happen. One of the staff would come in pretending he was just saying goodnight and then select one of the little kids and the filth would start. Some of those kids were only about nine or ten years old. The beatings I witnessed were terrible too. How these people got these jobs was beyond me. Those days, forty-five years ago, everything was 'hushed up' and it would be twenty years before the outside world faced up to the problem and accepted that for decades it had been the kids telling the truth and the wardens and staff who had been lying. I knew then that nobody would believe the kids if they complained. I was fortunate nobody tried anything on me… maybe it was because I was bigger and older and could handle myself.'

1956, aged sixteen Charlie turned more and more into a young gangster; but a gangster with a difference. One who will grow to live by his code of honour. He hates women beaters and child molesters. His presence becomes a constant challenge to the lowlife that prey on those who cannot defend themselves.

1957, at the age of seventeen, he mastered the art of safe blowing; which at the time was considered the pinnacle of excellence amongst the top criminal fraternity; and they gave him their respect. He was eventually arrested and remanded to an adult prison. As the crime was serious and high profile; high-ranking police officers from different parts of the country where safe-blowing crimes had taken place, came to interrogate him, (which in those days, was severe), but he refused their requests to talk.

At the High Court in the city of Chester, he stood charged with this serious offence. The right honourable Mr Justice Castles; who presided over his case, was quoted as saying: 'He is like a young lion who had tasted his first blood.' But through a legal and a technical point at the trial, the seventeen year old Charlie Seiga walked out of the court free, and made history for being the youngest safe-blower in Great Britain!

In 1964 at twenty-two years of age, he served a prison sentence of two years in Walton Prison, Liverpool. It was alleged he was dangerously armed with a shot gun; it is said he kept a gang of men including a police officer at bay, whilst his gang escaped.

Quote from Charlie: 'To be honest when I entered the prison I had acquired a massive reputation, it gained me respect amongst the top cons, so with a bit of pull here and there I was given a cushy job.'

He was appointed work on the prison reception. One of his duties was to serve meals to the last person in Britain to be hanged! He recalls seeing the condemned prisoner (his name was Allen) arriving back from court having been sentenced to death, being taken to the condemned cell, and being the last person to speak to him.

Quote from Charlie: 'I remember saying to Allen "You'll be ok, you'll get your reprieve." He seemed confident because six months before; a man named Masters was in the same condemned cell and he got reprieved. Also at that time in 1964 capital punishment was about to be abolished.'

Allen though was unlucky... he was hanged!

On the morning of the hanging all the prisoners in Walton Prison went from uproar to complete silence. We all knew that he was dead. After about an hour all our cells were unlocked; a friend of mine who was a cleaner told me he had been ordered to clean out the condemned cell; he told me it had been in a terrible mess there were blood stains on the walls and some of the furniture was broken. Later on one of the screws told us that Allen had put up a ferocious fight. I believe what used to happen was that if the condemned man struggled or tried to resist there would be a gang of screws as a back-up, who also assisted the hangman.

In the late 1960's and 70's Charlie became one of the most successful villains of his time. Police believed he was the brains behind the major firms involved in bank raids, wage snatches armed robberies and other serious crimes involving hundreds of thousands of pounds, but they remained unable to convict him; he became known as the 'Houdini' of the criminal underworld.

In the 1980's and 90's, crime had rapidly changed, the old school type gangster had almost disappeared, a new breed of criminal had emerged; and the vast majority of these became ruthless in their activities. The gun became, and still is, the weapon of choice. Gangster wars had broken out amongst the criminal fraternity!

In 1998 he went on trial for murder; he was accused of pumping three bullets into the head of one of these new lowlife breeds. He had also been questioned over other killings which were swift, brutal and brilliantly organised.

Quote from Charlie: 'It is quite true that I have been accused of killing other men and questioned about unsolved contract killings; the Liverpool Murder Squad, in their eyes still believe I was responsible. But they are wrong.'

Quote from the trial judge: 'This is a classic case of a contract killing.'

He was acquitted. No one has ever been convicted of the murder.

CROWN COURT

Regina V Charles Seiga

Particulars in Support of Reg. 9 (5) (B)

This was all in all as gruelling and hard-fought a murder trial as any I can remember in my 27 years at the criminal bar, in which time I have defended in literally dozens of important murder trials. This was a trial which demanded long hours of preparation at nights, weekends and in the early mornings in my hotel room to prepare for cross examination.

It was a dramatic and even a thrilling case. Nobody present will ever forget its atmosphere or the scenes of pandemonium in the public gallery which accompanied the final not guilty verdict.

This trial lasted 19 working days in all and I have to say I under-estimated both its length and factual difficulties at the outset. This was, in summary, in the very top league of contested murder trials in this country.

Jonathan Goldberg
3/11/98

CONFIDENTIAL POLICE MEMO

Liverpool Police Force 1998

Charles Antony Seiga - D.O.B. 7/4/1940

Charlie Seiga had a reputation for being a violent character. Intelligence was constantly being received of shootings being perpetrated by this man, but rarely would anyone come forward to complain about him.

He was known to be a careful planner and always seemed to provide a back door for himself when he knew he was to be arrested. He would often disappear after such events, and when the heat died down, would calmly walk into a police station and give himself up, knowing full well that the complaint had either been withdrawn or that the complainant, through fear, had been bought off.

He would vent his violence on other criminals who harmed or tried to bully his family or friends.

Having left the police force and now retired, it came as no surprise to me when I read about Seiga being arrested for a contract killing. How he got out of that one I do not know, and the secret of that job, along with many others, will no doubt be carried with him to his grave. The police are not looking for anyone else in relation to this matter and, in my experience; they must be more than satisfied that they had the correct man in the dock.

He was commonly known as Charlie Seiga, but we had another name for him - Killer!

Charlie Seiga became the longest reigning gangster in Great Britain; stretching from the 50's right up to the late 90's. He retired from a life of crime a few years ago; he is now reformed and a successful crime writer.

His books are still selling strongly today; as they will never date, and they are relevant to today's society.

Charlie Seiga has always been an enemy of and hates the lowlife in society who perpetrate such vile acts as rapists, women beaters and child molesters.

A script is currently being written based on this unique, eventful and powerful life story!

JUST A NOTE: All these hard hitting true stories and more can be read in Charlie Seiga's book titles:

KILLER
A LIVERPOOL STREETWISE KID
THE HYENAS
A KILLER VIGILANTE
LIVERPOOL'S NOTORIOUS JELLY GANG

A BRIEF SYNOPSIS OF CHARLIE SEIGA'S OTHER BOOKS

KILLER

By Charlie Seiga

Charlie Seiga was one of the most dangerous faces of the criminal underworld. There were many unsolved killings which were swift, brutal and brilliantly organised. The victims - liberty takers and sadists - were all hard bastards who dealt in the most vicious kind of violence. Many times the police marked him out as the vicious contract killer.

He was also one of the most successful villains of his time. Police believed that he was the brains behind major firms involved in robberies on banks, security vans, lorry hijacking, safe breaking and many other serious crimes. He lost track of the times he was arrested and questioned about various jobs, but he always had an alibi - a witness to say he wasn't guilty of the crime. He was the Houdini of the criminal underworld.

His story is a shocking tale of violence and crime; but it is also a story about one man's fight against the scum who break his deadly code of honour. He hates women beaters and child molesters.

His presence was a constant challenge to the low life that preyed on those who could not defend themselves.

It is an incredible autobiography of one of the most notorious figures in the history of British crime.

A LIVERPOOL STREETWISE KID

By Charlie Seiga

Times were hard in the 1940's and early 1950's. Kids went hungry and food was rationed. Some families had to beg, steal or borrow to survive. There seemed no way out for some kids, but Charlie found his own way out. On a routine basis he and his child gang plundered every shop they came across, robbing them of their food to put on the family table and their goods to sell on.

At the age of thirteen and always bunking off school, he went on to make further progress in his way of life. With his baby face and dressed as an office boy in blazer, shirt and tie, he was darting in and out of the office buildings in the city centre of Liverpool, raiding their cash draws and safes.

Quote from Charlie: 'We had one of the best little firms in Huyton, we got up to all kinds of things; fighting, robbery, you name it. Nobody could stop us or so I thought. I was scared of nothing and of nobody; especially the bizzies (police). In 1954 and at the tender age of fourteen I was earning more money than a professional adult. I was the richest, poor teenager in Liverpool.'

A Streetwise Kid is a brilliant combination of narrative writing, memoir and biography. A true story of a childhood villain and his young gang growing up in war torn Liverpool.

A KILLER VIGILANTE

By Charlie Seiga

A major breakdown in society has descended, and everything is spiralling out of control on council ghettos across the city. The police don't have the ability to deal with it and are demoralised. The streets are lawless. Marauding gangs are committing the vilest acts imaginable: rapes, violence against old people, arson attacks on family homes and gun crime. Unfortunately, decent hard working people live amongst it all. It is an unbearable existence for them, until John Christian, who was born and bred on the council estate many years before, comes up with a solution to the problem. After recruiting and forming his own crew; their belief was that the low-life scum who terrorise the women, kids, old and infirm should be terrorised themselves in a more frightening manner than they could ever 1mag1ne.

Their presence on the streets becomes a constant challenge to the lowlife and when the team happen to capture any of these vile yobs, the justice they inflict on the scum is swift, brutal and brilliantly organised.

They become known as vigilantes who sheriff their own community. This book contains violence in the most graphic detail.

REVIEWS OF CHARLIE SEIGA'S OTHER BOOKS

'A Liverpool Streetwise Kid'

After reading Charlie's first book Killer I couldn't wait to get my hands on this new title. I read it cover to cover without stopping for breath. The life story of Charlie's childhood years growing up in Liverpool and learning his criminal trade was both fascinating, funny and sad. This book left me crying and laughing at the true stories he tells page after page. I highly recommend this book as a must read!
Fred, Amazon UK

A brilliant combination of narrative writing, memoir and biography.
Kevin Bryan, Publisher, Cumbria

Wow! What a read! After reading Charlies first book Killer I couldn't wait to get my hands on this new title. I read it cover to cover without stopping for breath. The life story of Charlies childhood years growing up in Liverpool and learning his crim-inal trade was both fascinating, funny and sad. This book left me crying and laughing at the true stories he tells page after page. I highly recommend this book as a must read!
Sarah Johnson, St Helens

Fabulously real narrative! A Kid's Review! Charlie's childhood could never be described as dull and ordinary. He and his family found themselves needing, and Charlie went out there and provide...any way he could! This book is a true gem. The descriptions of the environment in war torn Liverpool will ring bells for many others who suffered and lived through the hard times of yesteryear. And those who were lucky enough not to will get a unique insight into the true way it was! It is sensitive, moving, funny and truly entertaining. This wonderful book is a social history as well as an autobiography; real page turner and a story you can read again and again. It is not unlike a modern day Oliver Twist! Any money spent on buying this book will be money well spent. If only all autobiographies were this honest and raw straight from the horse's mouth. FABULOUS BOOK FABULOUS AUTHOR!!

A. Customer. Amazon UK

Fascinating! The early years autobiography of Charlie Seiga, one of Liverpool's most notorious criminals and author of 'Killers' and 'The Hyenas'. This fascinating book tells how his life of crime began and is in turn sensitive, moving, funny as well as spelling out his villainous ways, always with a strict code of honour. A very scarce book.

Godfry Books

The huckleberry fin of Liverpool! This book is such an unusual narrative for these days, as it is of a 'child' gangster for the want of a better word. Charlie Seiga was just 12 years old when he turned to crime to provide food and other basics for the large family he was from. He starts off just stealing food and sweets but then after meeting his mentor; a thirty odd year old woman who teaches him all she knows about blagging and thieving on a more lucrative level. Charlie Seiga writes about his younger years after writing his first book Killer and getting asked to write in more detail about his childhood. And so as requested here is A Liverpool Streetwise Kid...all the ups and downs, and sad and funny tails of the 'Huckleberry Fin' of (too many line spaces here Jane)Liverpool. Highly recommended. Buy it and read it, you won't be disappointed...5 Star!!!

A Customer

'A Killer Vigilante'

A KILLER VIGILANTE is an exciting read and would make a good film. It is interesting and well written. Some scenes even show off Charlie's sensitive, emotional side. It is written in a very gripping, vivid style, and what impresses me most is the visual power of Charlie's narration; I can really visualise the places, people and situations - it is almost like being there!

Prof Tomasz Pobog-Malinowski
- Professor Emeritus, Media, Edge Hill University
- Visiting Professor, Film Production, University of Lincoln
Producer-Director Flying Brick Films

Gripping! I had to sit and finish this book once I started it as I just couldn't put it down. Well written, and totally gripping. I can't wait to read his other stuff1

Laura C from Newton-Le-Willows

Masterpiece! This is another masterpiece by local author Charlie Seiga. It is a fantastic gripping story which I read in one day as I could not put it down. A real feel good story knowing that the bad guys got their just desserts. I would actually say that this is my favourite book by Charlie (and I have read them all) and I hope that he brings out a sequel as I would love to read that too. His writing is gritty and sometimes quite gruesome but true to the story. I have recommended this book to many of my friends and bought several as Christmas presents and the response has been great. Everyone loved it. Keep the good work up Charlie.

Lynch

Surprisingly philosophical! Charlie doesn't only tell a good story but he is very philosophical about things. He highlights the turmoil of the country, very topical at the moment with the current rebellions and the like. He talks of how the people in power let our countrymen down. Charlie Seiga's books and Vigilante in particular were recommended to me as I study social behaviour and the deprivation of some of society, and having read it; I now have no hesitation in recommending this book to everyone.

Roger Emmington, London

Excellent! Gripping, realistic and graphic! This is by far the best crime book I have read in years! Charlie Seiga will be the next big Crime writer of this decade! Great read from an ex pat here in Australia!!! This is a must read!! I have read his other true crime books and this is another hit!

Paul Mc from Australia

Powerful Story! I wasn't sure if I would like this book as it said it was very graphically brutal but it was recommended to me and I thought I would give it a go. It was a great story that kept me interested right to the end and that must be good because usually I start a book but don't finish it as I am not a big reader. It is really, really brutal but only the scum bags get hurt and right from the beginning you are on the side of John Christian. It is shocking to think that in some areas of the north-west these things are actually going on; on a daily basis. The Vigilantes do all they can to even the balance in favour of the victims and I wouldn't be surprised if this story made people think about standing up for themselves and beating the bullies at their own game. It is definitely a book that will get people talking and debating, I would highly recommend 'Vigilante' to everyone old or young, man or woman, you will be hooked from the start. I hope there is a sequel to this title and it would make a brilliant film.

Sammijaz From Cheshire

Good Work Charlie! It's a rare thing when after finishing a book you immediately go back to the beginning and start again. That was the case with Charlie Seiga's Vigilante. I never wanted it to end, so it earned itself a second read, which was exactly what I did. I've read some of Seiga's books before, Killer being one of my favourites, but Vigilante is up with there with the best of them. What makes it stand out from others is how real and robust it is. Nothing is left to the imagination and it's clear that Seiga has experienced firsthand what goes on in its pages. Not since Paul Schrader and Martin Scorsese teamed up to make the all-time classic Taxi Driver has a book of this type grabbed my attention so much. It was 1976 when De Niro hit our screens with his unmistakable portrayal of Travis Bickle. That was then and this is now, now is the time for Vigilante. Get it bought and get it read. You won't be disappointed.

Russ B from Gloucestershire

Violent... But Riveting Took this book home to Egypt and started and, finished it on the plane. It is riveting from the start. Vigilante is a brutal but truly compelling story about hitting back at the low life that are a blight on the lives of good, honest and decent people. The scum though get their just desserts. The good guys going after the bad guys; we could do with more of this to sort out and re-claim the streets and housing estates in England! Although a 'fictional' book about Liverpool vigilantes; it sounds very true to life to me!

KB from Hurghada, Egypt

Impressive! I read Charlie Seiga's new release Vigilante; it is certainly an impressive piece of work; totally convincing and up to a point the reader can empathise with John Christian. The violence although vividly described, is a necessary part of this story. However, the narrative is not all about brutal violence; it is also a good descriptive read.

Bert H from London

Awesome! I haven't read a book cover to cover for two years, despite trying several different ones every week - they simply did not hold my attention and grip me enough to want to finish them. Vigilante, however, I read within two days - I can only say that it is absolutely awesome! It is certainly close to the bone in parts, and not for the squeamish, in terms of the violence; but throughout the story, the reader is told why it is being dished out! If you are a fan of crime and thriller books, this is simply the best out there. In short if this is the genre you are into, you simply MUST read it! You will not be disappointed. Charlie Seiga has written a crime novel that will become a classic - I doubt if it will ever die out.

JR from Formby

Vigilante which I received a couple of days ago .... can't put it down!! The story is infectious and gripping.

Scott Cameron, Liverpool

OTHER BOOKS BY GADFLY PRESS

By John G Sutton:
HMP Manchester Prison Officer: I Survived Terrorists, Murderers, Rapists and Freemason Officer Attacks in Strangeways and Wormwood Scrubs

By Lee Marvin Hitchman:
How I Survived Shootings, Stabbings, Prison, Crack Addiction, Manchester Gangs and Dog Attacks

By William Rodríguez Abadía:
Son of the Cali Cartel: The Narcos Who Wiped Out Pablo Escobar and the Medellín Cartel

By Chet Sandhu:
Self-Made, Dues Paid: An Asian Kid Who Became an International Drug-Smuggling Gangster

By Kaz B:
Confessions of a Dominatrix: My Secret BDSM Life

By Peter McAleese:
Killing Escobar and Soldier Stories

By Joe Egan:
Big Joe Egan: The Toughest White Man on the Planet

By Anthony Valentine:
Britain's No. 1 Art Forger Max Brandrett: The Life of a Cheeky Faker

By Johnnyboy Steele:
Scotland's Johnnyboy: The Bird That Never Flew

By Ian 'Blink' MacDonald:
Scotland's Wildest Bank Robber: Guns, Bombs and Mayhem in Glasgow's Gangland

By Michael Sheridan:
The Murder of Sophie: How I Hunted and Haunted the West Cork Killer

By Steve Wraith:
The Krays' Final Years: My Time with London's Most Iconic Gangsters

By Natalie Welsh:
Escape from Venezuela's Deadliest Prison

By Shaun Attwood:
English Shaun Trilogy
Party Time
Hard Time
Prison Time

War on Drugs Series

Pablo Escobar: Beyond Narcos
American Made: Who Killed Barry Seal? Pablo Escobar or George HW Bush
The Cali Cartel: Beyond Narcos
Clinton Bush and CIA Conspiracies: From the Boys on the Tracks to Jeffrey Epstein
Who Killed Epstein? Prince Andrew or Bill Clinton

Un-Making a Murderer: The Framing of Steven Avery and Brendan Dassey
The Mafia Philosopher: Two Tonys
Life Lessons

Pablo Escobar's Story (4-book series)

By Johnnyboy Steele:

Scotland's Johnnyboy: The Bird That Never Flew

"A cross between *Shawshank Redemption* and *Escape from Alcatraz!*" – Shaun Attwood, YouTuber and Author

All his life, 'Johnnyboy' Steele has been running. Firstly, from an abusive father, then from the rigours of an approved school and a young offenders jail, and, finally, from the harshness of adult prison. This book details how the Steele brothers staged the most daring breakout that Glasgow's Barlinnie prison had ever seen and recounts what happened when their younger brother, Joseph, was falsely accused of the greatest mass murder in Scottish legal history.

If Johnnyboy had wings, he would have flown to help his family, but he would have to wait for freedom to use his expertise to publicise young Joe's miscarriage of justice.

This is a compelling, often shocking and uncompromisingly honest account of how the human spirit can survive against almost crushing odds. It is a story of family love, friendship and, ultimately, a desire for justice.

By Ian 'Blink' MacDonald:

Scotland's Wildest Bank Robber: Guns, Bombs and Mayhem in Glasgow's Gangland

As a young man in Glasgow's underworld, Ian 'Blink' MacDonald earned a reputation for fighting and stabbing his enemies. After refusing to work for Arthur "The Godfather" Thompson, he attempted to steal £6 million in a high-risk armed bank robbery. While serving 16 years, Blink met the torture-gang boss Eddie Richardson, the serial killer Archie Hall, notorious lifer Charles Bronson and members of the Krays.

After his release, his drug-fuelled violent lifestyle created conflict with the police and rival gangsters. Rearrested several times, he was the target of a gruesome assassination attempt. During filming for Danny Dyer's Deadliest Men, a bomb was discovered under Blink's car and the terrified camera crew members fled from Scotland.

In *Scotland's Wildest Bank Robber*, Blink provides an eye-opening account of how he survived gangland warfare, prisons, stabbings and bombs.

By Michael Sheridan:

The Murder of Sophie: How I Hunted and Haunted the West Cork Killer

Just before Christmas, 1996, a beautiful French woman – the wife of a movie mogul – was brutally murdered outside of her holiday home in a remote region of West Cork, Ireland. The crime was reported by a local journalist, Ian Bailey, who was at the forefront of the case until he became the prime murder suspect. Arrested twice, he was released without charge.

This was the start of a saga lasting decades with twists and turns and a battle for justice in two countries, which culminated in the 2019 conviction of Bailey – in his absence – by the French Criminal court in Paris. But it was up to the Irish courts to decide whether he would be extradited to serve a 25-year prison sentence.

With the unrivalled co-operation of major investigation sources and the backing of the victim's family, the author unravels the shocking facts of a unique murder case.

By Steve Wraith:

The Krays' Final Years:
My Time with London's Most Iconic Gangsters

Britain's most notorious twins – Ron and Reg Kray – ascended the underworld to become the most feared and legendary gangsters in London. Their escalating mayhem culminated in murder, for which they received life sentences in 1969.

While incarcerated, they received letters from a schoolboy from Tyneside, Steve Wraith, who was mesmerised by their story. Eventually, Steve visited them in prison and a friendship formed. The Twins hired Steve as an unofficial advisor, which brought him into contact with other members of their crime family. At Ron's funeral, Steve was Charlie Kray's right-hand man.

Steve documents Ron's time in Broadmoor – a high-security psychiatric hospital – where he was battling insanity and heavily medicated. Steve details visiting Reg, who served almost 30 years in a variety of prisons, where the gangster was treated with the utmost respect by the staff and the inmates.

By Natalie Welsh:

Escape from Venezuela's Deadliest Prison

After getting arrested at a Venezuelan airport with a suitcase of cocaine, Natalie was clueless about the danger she was facing. Sentenced to 10 years, she arrived at a prison with armed men on the roof, whom she mistakenly believed were the guards, only to find out they were homicidal gang members. Immediately, she was plunged into a world of unimaginable horror and escalating violence, where murder, rape and all-out gang warfare were carried out with the complicity of corrupt guards. Male prisoners often entered the women's housing area, bringing gunfire with them and leaving corpses behind. After 4.5 years, Natalie risked everything to escape and flee through Colombia, with the help of a guard who had fallen deeply in love with her.

By Shaun Attwood:

Pablo Escobar: Beyond Narcos

War on Drugs Series Book 1

The mind-blowing true story of Pablo Escobar and the Medellín Cartel, beyond their portrayal on Netflix.

Colombian drug lord Pablo Escobar was a devoted family man and a psychopathic killer; a terrible enemy, yet a wonderful friend. While donating millions to the poor, he bombed and tortured his enemies – some had their eyeballs removed with hot spoons. Through ruthless cunning and America's insatiable appetite for cocaine, he became a multi-billionaire, who lived in a $100-million house with its own zoo.

Pablo Escobar: Beyond Narcos demolishes the standard good versus evil telling of his story. The authorities were not hunting Pablo down to stop his cocaine business. They were taking it over.

American Made: Who Killed Barry Seal? Pablo Escobar or George HW Bush

War on Drugs Series Book 2

Set in a world where crime and government coexist, *American Made* is the jaw-dropping true story of CIA pilot Barry Seal that the Hollywood movie starring Tom Cruise is afraid to tell.

Barry Seal flew cocaine and weapons worth billions of dollars into and out of America in the 1980s. After he became a government informant, Pablo Escobar's Medellin Cartel offered a million for him alive and half a million dead. But his real trouble began after he threatened to expose the dirty dealings of George HW Bush.

American Made rips the roof off Bush and Clinton's complicity in cocaine trafficking in Mena, Arkansas.

"A conspiracy of the grandest magnitude." Congressman Bill Alexander on the Mena affair.

The Cali Cartel: Beyond Narcos

War on Drugs Series Book 3

An electrifying account of the Cali Cartel, beyond its portrayal on Netflix.

From the ashes of Pablo Escobar's empire rose an even bigger and more malevolent cartel. A new breed of sophisticated mobsters became the kings of cocaine. Their leader was Gilberto Rodríguez Orejuela – known as the Chess Player, due to his foresight and calculated cunning.

Gilberto and his terrifying brother, Miguel, ran a multi-billion-dollar drug empire like a corporation. They employed a politically astute brand of thuggery and spent $10 million to put a president in power. Although the godfathers from Cali preferred bribery over violence, their many loyal torturers and hitmen were never idle.

Clinton, Bush and CIA Conspiracies: From the Boys on the Tracks to Jeffrey Epstein

War on Drugs Series Book 4

In the 1980s, George HW Bush imported cocaine to finance an illegal war in Nicaragua. Governor Bill Clinton's Arkansas state police provided security for the drug drops. For assisting the CIA, the Clinton Crime Family was awarded the White House. The #clintonbodycount continues to this day, with the deceased including Jeffrey Epstein.

This book features harrowing true stories that reveal the insanity of the drug war. A mother receives the worst news about her son. A journalist gets a tip that endangers his life. An unemployed man becomes California's biggest crack dealer. A DEA agent in Mexico is sacrificed for going after the big players.

The lives of Linda Ives, Gary Webb, Freeway Rick Ross and Kiki Camarena are shattered by brutal experiences. Not all of them will survive.

Pablo Escobar's Story (4-book series)

"Finally, the definitive book about Escobar, original and up-to-date." – UNILAD

"The most comprehensive account ever written." – True Geordie

Pablo Escobar was a mama's boy, who cherished his family and sang in the shower, yet he bombed a passenger plane and formed a death squad that used genital electrocution.

Most Escobar biographies only provide a few pieces of the puzzle, but this action-packed 1000-page book reveals everything about the king of cocaine.

Mostly translated from Spanish, Part 1 contains stories untold in the English-speaking world, including:

The tragic death of his youngest brother, Fernando.

The fate of his pregnant mistress.

The shocking details of his affair with a TV celebrity.

The presidential candidate who encouraged him to eliminate their rivals.

The Mafia Philosopher

"A fast-paced true-crime memoir with all of the action of Goodfellas." – UNILAD

"Sopranos v Sons of Anarchy with an Alaskan-snow backdrop." – True Geordie Podcast

Breaking bones, burying bodies and planting bombs became second nature to Two Tonys, while working for the Bonanno Crime Family, whose exploits inspired The Godfather.

After a dispute with an outlaw motorcycle club, Two Tonys left a trail of corpses from Arizona to Alaska. On the run, he was pursued by bikers and a neo-Nazi gang, blood-thirsty for revenge, while a homicide detective launched a nationwide manhunt.

As the mist from his smoking gun fades, readers are left with an unexpected portrait of a stoic philosopher with a wealth of charm, a glorious turn of phrase and a fanatical devotion to his daughter.

Party Time

An action-packed roller-coaster account of a life spiralling out of control, featuring wild women, gangsters and a mountain of drugs.

Shaun Attwood arrived in Phoenix, Arizona, a penniless business graduate from a small industrial town in England. Within a decade, he became a stock-market millionaire. But he was leading a double life.

After taking his first ecstasy pill at a rave in Manchester as a shy student, Shaun became intoxicated by the party lifestyle that would change his fortune. Years later, in the Arizona desert, he became submerged in a criminal underworld, throwing parties for thousands of ravers and running an ecstasy ring in competition with the Mafia mass murderer, Sammy 'The Bull' Gravano.

As greed and excess tore through his life, Shaun had eye-watering encounters with Mafia hitmen and crystal-meth addicts, enjoyed extravagant debauchery with superstar DJs and glitter girls, and ingested enough drugs to kill a herd of elephants. This is his story.

Hard Time

"Makes the Shawshank Redemption look like a holiday camp."
– NOTW

After a SWAT team smashed down stock-market millionaire Shaun Attwood's door, he found himself inside Arizona's deadliest jail and locked into a brutal struggle for survival.

Shaun's hope of living the American Dream turned into a nightmare of violence and chaos, when he had a run-in with Sammy "the Bull" Gravano, an Italian Mafia mass murderer.

In jail, Shaun was forced to endure cockroaches crawling in his ears at night, dead rats in the food and the sound of skulls getting cracked against toilets. He meticulously documented the conditions and smuggled out his message.

Join Shaun on a harrowing voyage into the darkest recesses of human existence.

Hard Time provides a revealing glimpse into the tragedy, brutality, dark comedy and eccentricity of prison life.

Featured worldwide on Nat Geo Channel's Locked-Up/ Banged-Up Abroad Raving Arizona.

Prison Time

Sentenced to 9½ years in Arizona's state prison for distributing ecstasy, Shaun finds himself living among gang members, sexual predators and drug-crazed psychopaths. After being attacked by a Californian biker, in for stabbing a girlfriend, Shaun writes about the prisoners who befriend, protect and inspire him. They include T-Bone, a massive African American ex-Marine, who risks his life saving vulnerable inmates from rape, and Two Tonys, an old-school Mafia murderer, who left the corpses of his rivals from Arizona to Alaska. They teach Shaun how to turn incarceration to his advantage, and to learn from his mistakes.

Shaun is no stranger to love and lust in the heterosexual world, but the tables are turned on him inside. Sexual advances come at him from all directions, some cleverly disguised, others more sinister.

Resigned to living alongside violent, mentally ill and drug-ad-dicted inmates, Shaun immerses himself in psychology and philosophy, to try to make sense of his past behaviour, and begins applying what he learns, as he adapts to prison life. Encouraged by Two Tonys to explore fiction as well, Shaun reads over 1000 books which, with support from a brilliant psychotherapist, Dr Owen, speed along his personal development. As his ability to deflect daily threats improves, Shaun begins to look forward to his release with optimism and a new love waiting for him. Yet the words of Aristotle from one of Shaun's books will prove prophetic: "We cannot learn without pain."

Un-Making a Murderer:
The Framing of Steven Avery and Brendan Dassey

Innocent people do go to jail. Sometimes mistakes are made. But even more terrifying is when the authorities conspire to frame them. That's what happened to Steven Avery and Brendan Dassey, who were convicted of murder and are serving life sentences.

Un-Making a Murderer is an explosive book, which uncovers the illegal, devious and covert tactics used by Wisconsin officials, including:

– Concealing Other Suspects

– Paying Expert Witnesses to Lie

– Planting Evidence

– Jury Tampering

The art of framing innocent people has been in practice for centuries and will continue until the perpetrators are held accountable. Turning conventional assumptions and beliefs in the justice system upside down, *Un-Making a Murderer* takes you on that journey.

HARD TIME BY SHAUN ATTWOOD
CHAPTER 1

Sleep deprived and scanning for danger, I enter a dark cell on the second floor of the maximum-security Madison Street jail in Phoenix, Arizona, where guards and gang members are murdering prisoners. Behind me, the metal door slams heavily. Light slants into the cell through oblong gaps in the door, illuminating a prisoner cocooned in a white sheet, snoring lightly on the top bunk about two thirds of the way up the back wall. Relieved there is no immediate threat, I place my mattress on the grimy floor. Desperate to rest, I notice movement on the cement-block walls. *Am I hallucinating?* I blink several times. The walls appear to ripple. Stepping closer, I see the walls are alive with insects. I flinch. So many are swarming, I wonder if they're a colony of ants on the move. To get a better look, I put my eyes right up to them. They are mostly the size of almonds and have antennae. American cockroaches. I've seen them in the holding cells downstairs in smaller numbers, but nothing like this. A chill spread over my body. I back away.

Something alive falls from the ceiling and bounces off the base of my neck. I jump. With my night vision improving, I spot cockroaches weaving in and out of the base of the fluorescent strip light. Every so often one drops onto the concrete and resumes crawling. Examining the bottom bunk, I realise why my cellmate is sleeping at a higher elevation: cockroaches are pouring from gaps in the decrepit wall at the level of my bunk. The area is thick with them. Placing my mattress on the bottom bunk scatters them. I walk towards the toilet, crunching a few under my shower sandals. I urinate and grab the toilet roll. A cockroach darts from the centre of the roll onto my hand, tickling my fingers. My arm jerks as if it has a mind of its own, losing the cockroach and the toilet roll. Using a towel, I wipe the bulk of them off the bottom bunk, stopping only to shake the odd one off my hand. I unroll my mattress. They begin to regroup and inhabit my mattress. My adrenaline is pumping so much, I lose my fatigue.

Nauseated, I sit on a tiny metal stool bolted to the wall. *How will I sleep? How's my cellmate sleeping through the infestation and my arrival?* Copying his technique, I cocoon myself in a sheet and lie down, crushing more cockroaches. The only way they can access me now is through the breathing hole I've left in the sheet by the lower half of my face. Inhaling their strange musty odour, I close my eyes. I can't sleep. I feel them crawling on the sheet around my feet. *Am I imagining things?* Frightened of them infiltrating my breathing hole, I keep opening my eyes. Cramps cause me to rotate onto my other side. Facing the wall, I'm repulsed by so many of them just inches away. I return to my original side.

The sheet traps the heat of the Sonoran Desert to my body, soaking me in sweat. Sweat tickles my body, tricking my mind into thinking the cockroaches are infiltrating and crawling on me. The trapped heat aggravates my bleeding skin infections and bedsores. I want to scratch myself, but I know better. The outer layers of my skin have turned soggy from sweating constantly in this concrete oven. Squirming on the bunk fails to stop the relentless itchiness of my skin. Eventually, I scratch myself. Clumps of moist skin detach under my nails. Every now and then I become so uncomfortable, I must open my cocoon to waft the heat out, which allows the cockroaches in. It takes hours to drift to sleep. I only manage a few hours. I awake stuck to the soaked sheet, disgusted by the cockroach carcasses compressed against the mattress.

The cockroaches plague my new home until dawn appears at the dots in the metal grid over a begrimed strip of four-inch-thick bullet-proof glass at the top of the back wall – the cell's only source of outdoor light. They disappear into the cracks in the walls, like vampire mist retreating from sunlight. But not all of them. There were so many on the night shift that even their vastly reduced number is too many to dispose of. And they act like they know it. They roam around my feet with attitude, as if to make it clear that I'm trespassing on their turf.

My next set of challenges will arise not from the insect world, but from my neighbours. I'm the new arrival, subject to scrutiny about my charges just like when I'd run into the Aryan Brotherhood prison gang on my first day at the medium-security Towers jail a year ago. I wish my cellmate would wake up, brief me on the mood of the locals and introduce me to the head of the white gang. No such luck. Chow is announced over a speaker system in a crackly robotic voice, but he doesn't stir.

I emerge into the day room for breakfast. Prisoners in black-and-white bee-striped uniforms gather under the metal-grid stairs and tip dead cockroaches into a trash bin from plastic peanut-butter containers they'd set as traps during the night. All eyes are on me in the chow line. Watching who sits where, I hold my head up, put on a solid stare and pretend to be as at home in this environment as the cockroaches. It's all an act. I'm lonely and afraid. I loathe having to explain myself to the head of the white race, who I assume is the toughest murderer. I've been in jail long enough to know that taking my breakfast to my cell will imply that I have something to hide.

The gang punishes criminals with certain charges. The most serious are sex offenders, who are KOS: Kill On Sight. Other charges are punishable by SOS – Smash On Sight – such as drive-by shootings because women and kids sometimes get killed. It's called convict justice. Gang members are constantly looking for people to beat up because that's how they earn their reputations and tattoos. The most serious acts of violence earn the highest-ranking tattoos. To be a full gang member requires murder. I've observed the body language and techniques inmates trying to integrate employ. An inmate with a spring in his step and an air of confidence is likely to be accepted. A person who avoids eye contact and fails to introduce himself to the gang is likely to be preyed on. Some of the failed attempts I saw ended up with heads getting cracked against toilets, a sound I've grown familiar with. I've seen prisoners being extracted on stretchers who looked dead – one had yellow fluid leaking from his head. The constant violence gives me nightmares, but the reality is that I put myself in here, so I force myself to accept it as a part of my punishment.

It's time to apply my knowledge. With a self-assured stride, I take my breakfast bag to the table of white inmates covered in neo-Nazi tattoos, allowing them to question me.

"Mind if I sit with you guys?" I ask, glad exhaustion has deepened my voice.

"These seats are taken. But you can stand at the corner of the table."

The man who answered is probably the head of the gang. I size him up. Cropped brown hair. A dangerous glint in Nordic-blue eyes. Tiny pupils that suggest he's on heroin. Weightlifter-type veins bulging from a sturdy neck. Political ink on arms crisscrossed with scars. About the same age as me, thirty-three.

"Thanks. I'm Shaun from England." I volunteer my origin to show I'm different from them but not in a way that might get me smashed.

"I'm Bullet, the head of the whites." He offers me his fist to bump. "Where you roll in from, wood?"

Addressing me as wood is a good sign. It's what white gang members on a friendly basis call each other.

"Towers jail. They increased my bond and re-classified me to maximum security."

"What's your bond at?"

"I've got two $750,000 bonds," I say in a monotone. This is no place to brag about bonds.

"How many people you kill, brother?" His eyes drill into mine, checking whether my body language supports my story. My body language so far is spot on.

"None. I threw rave parties. They got us talking about drugs on wiretaps." Discussing drugs on the phone does not warrant a $1.5 million bond. I know and beat him to his next question. "Here's my charges." I show him my charge sheet, which includes conspiracy and leading a crime syndicate – both from running an Ecstasy ring.

Bullet snatches the paper and scrutinises it. Attempting to pre-empt his verdict, the other whites study his face. On edge, I wait for him to respond. Whatever he says next will determine whether I'll be accepted or victimised.

"Are you some kind of jailhouse attorney?" Bullet asks. "I want someone to read through my case paperwork." During our few minutes of conversation, Bullet has seen through my act and concluded that I'm educated – a possible resource to him.

I appreciate that he'll accept me if I take the time to read his case. "I'm no jailhouse attorney, but I'll look through it and help you however I can."

"Good. I'll stop by your cell later on, wood."

After breakfast, I seal as many of the cracks in the walls as I can with toothpaste. The cell smells minty, but the cockroaches still find their way in. Their day shift appears to be collecting information on the brown paper bags under my bunk, containing a few items of food that I purchased from the commissary; bags that I tied off with rubber bands in the hope of keeping the cockroaches out. Relentlessly, the cockroaches explore the bags for entry points, pausing over and probing the most worn and vulnerable regions. *Will the nightly swarm eat right through the paper?* I read all morning, wondering whether my cellmate has died in his cocoon, his occasional breathing sounds reassuring me.

Bullet stops by late afternoon and drops his case paperwork off. He's been charged with Class 3 felonies and less, not serious crimes, but is facing a double-digit sentence because of his prior convictions and Security Threat Group status in the prison system. The proposed sentencing range seems disproportionate. I'll advise him to reject the plea bargain – on the assumption he